Until now, nearly all books about sex have been written for men about women—and how to make love to them successfully. This book is for women. Its purpose is to tell them about men and sex. Some of it is controversial.

The psychology of women often makes them more self-accepting, more in touch with their feelings, more open to new ideas and, more importantly, *better students* and *better teachers* of sex. To be a good teacher, one must know and understand the nature of her student. Only a better understanding *between* the sexes can insure a richer, more satisfying love life for both sexes.

Also by Dr. Theodore Isaac Rubin available now from Ballantine Books:

COMPASSION AND SELF-HATE: An Alternative to Despair *(with Eleanor Rubin)*

LISA AND DAVID/JORDI

UNDERSTANDING YOUR MAN:

A Woman's Guide

by Theodore Isaac Rubin, M.D.
and David C. Berliner

BALLANTINE BOOKS • NEW YORK

Library of Congress Catalog Card Number: 77-605

ISBN 0-345-26078-3

Manufactured in the United States of America

First Edition: October 1977

Contents

INTRODUCTION   Our Purpose   1
CHAPTER 1   THAT WHICH IS LEARNED   4
   The Family Influence and Sexual Attitudes   6
CHAPTER 2   MACHISMO!   13
   The Aura of Machismo   15
   Masculinity Symbols: Cultural Differences 17
   Hero Identification   18
   Sexual Prowess: Men Need a Passing Mark   20
CHAPTER 3   MEN'S FEARS   21
   "Love" Is Hard to Say   23
   Rejection   25
CHAPTER 4   DEPENDENCY   27
CHAPTER 5   DETACHMENT: FEARS OF INTI-
          MACY AND INVOLVEMENT   35
CHAPTER 6   WOMEN   39
   One Step Backward, Two Steps Ahead   41
   The Double Standard   45
   More on Orgasms   47
CHAPTER 7   OEDIPAL FEELING AND HOSTILITY   48
   Woman the Enforcer   49
   Boredom—What Cure?   51
   Why Can't I Do That?   53
CHAPTER 8   LITTLE BOYS   54
   The Need for Groups   56
   Temptations   58
CHAPTER 9   ANXIETY AND GUILT   59
   Guilt   62
CHAPTER 10   THE PENIS: SYMBOL, WEAPON,
          DELIGHT   64
   Early Roots   65
   A Look at the Facts   66
   Different Perspectives   69
   More of the Physical   72
   Erections   73
   Orgasms and Ejaculation   74
   Circumcision   78
   Castration   79
CHAPTER 11   HOMOSEXUALITY—LIFESTYLE/
          NIGHTMARE   81
   Homosexuality: Its Development   81
   Homosexuality to Heterosexuality   83
   Inner Feelings   85
   Talent and Homosexuality   86
   Appearance and Homosexuality   87
   Fear of Homosexuality   89
   Men and Childhood Pressure   91
   Fear of Discovery   93
   Displaying Affection   93
   Athletics and Masculinity   96

Muscle Men   97
Bisexuality   100
CHAPTER 12 SEX (BODY AND MIND)   102
Compartmentalization   103
The Don Juan Syndrome   105
Mechanical Differences   106
More about Erections   107
Sexual Positions: Their Meanings   108
Minor Problems   110
CHAPTER 13 SEXUAL PROBLEMS   112
Physical Causes of Impotence   113
Impotence of Emotional Origin   114
Surgery: The Facts   115
Chronic Emotional Impotence   116
Premature Ejaculation   118
Rarities   120
CHAPTER 14 FANTASIES   121
Types of Sex Fantasies   123
Origin and Purpose   124
Male and Female Fantasies Are Not the Same   126
Fantasizing: Its Complications   127
CHAPTER 15 MASTURBATION   131
Society: The Guilt Producer   132
The Female Reaction   133
Nocturnal Emissions   135
CHAPTER 16 PORNOGRAPHY   137
Picture or Pornography   138
Pornography as a Hobby   140
Conclusion   141
CHAPTER 17 COMPATABILITY   143
Experience and Frequency   145
Love-Hate   148
Men Are Romantics   149
The Faked Orgasm   150
Observations and Hints   152
CHAPTER 18 TRADITION, MARRIAGE AND
            BEYOND   155
Impact of a Child   158
CHAPTER 19 INFIDELITY   162
Temptations   163
Group Pressure   165
Men as Collectors   166
Prostitutes   168
Coping with Guilt   169
Swapping Partners   170
CHAPTER 20 MALE CLIMACTERIC   172
The Envy of Youth   175
Health and the Climacteric   176
Fear of Death   177
CHAPTER 21 THE NEW WOMAN   179
The Male: Added Expectations   180
Toward a Greater Understanding   181
Matriarchal versus Patriarchal   182
EPILOGUE   185

Introduction

Our Purpose

> The brain is viewed as an appendage of
> the genital glands.
> —Dr. Carl Jung on Freud's
> Theory of Sexuality

Until now, nearly all books about sex have been
written for men about women—and how to make love
to them successfully. There is little doubt that this
one-sided approach has been due to simplistic and
erroneous notions that men are the initiators, are more
experienced and self-assertive, and are better able to
comprehend anatomy, physiology and sexual gymnastics. Some books have been thinly disguised pornography hidden behind a respectable front but
intended solely to titillate both men and women readers. Unfortunately, very few books have dealt with
the crucial emotional aspects of sex, and most have
failed to discuss aspects that depart from pure sexual
mechanics.

This book is for women. Its purpose is to tell them
about men and sex. Sadly, many women are brought
up to be highly romantic and at the same time are fed
unrealistic notions about sex. Our culture sustains
much misinformation through ideas and half-truths
supplied by parents, books, songs, plays, movies and
television. Many women suffer from self-hate and
blame themselves for breakdowns in relationships because they lack understanding of male sexual psychology.

For the most part, this book is based on observation, clinical study and experience rather than opinion,

but it is virtually impossible for my interpretation not to play some role. Some of the things I have to say are controversial. In some issues I wish it were otherwise. I am convinced, for example, that the vast majority of men are greatly influenced by "little boy" aspects of themselves that they have been unable to escape. As a result, many men unconsciously seek sexual partners who will also be good mothers.

I also feel that most men are extremely dependent on women (even though they steadfastly refuse to concede that reliance) and often harbor considerable hostility toward the one they love and of women in general. Many and perhaps even the majority of American men fear and have confused notions regarding homosexuality.

Since this book is about the *men* in our time and culture, it unavoidably courts all the dangers inherent in generalizing. I still feel, however, that it applies to the majority of men in our population. Individual differences and modifications undoubtedly exist on socioeconomic, educational, familial and physiological levels. Age sometimes plays a role, especially when different generations are involved. But for the most part, I believe that the material is applicable with relatively minor modifications to account for individuality.

Why write a book for women about the sexual psychology of men? Our society unfortunately maximizes male pride and produces blocking and closure to any material not to a man's liking. (I shall deal with material related to male pride later on in this book.) Suffice it to say here that the psychology of women—regardless of whether the origin of its development be physiological, cultural or both—makes them, all other things being equal (education, sociocultural background, age, experience, etc.), more self-accepting, more in touch with their feelings, more open to new ideas, better able to ask for professional help and, most important, *better students* and *better teachers* of sex. I also feel women are more complicated and highly developed than men in the psychosexual areas. Their satisfaction is based on more complex needs than men's.

Many men retain the illusion that they are more knowledgeable about sex, and also believe that they alone are responsible for pleasure and satisfaction either attained or frustrated in *both* partners. Actually, many women use subliminal cues to initiate sex. They tell him *when* but unfortunately not *how*. Many women know how, and if they don't, there are any number of good sexual manuals written about women for men. Many men have read these manuals, yet still remain inadequate sexual practitioners. It is not enough for a woman to know the material written about herself, however thorough and instructive it may be. To be a good teacher (and I am convinced that if no serious problems exist, her ability as a good teacher is what makes the difference between a relatively good and a poor sexual relationship), she must know and understand the nature of her student. In this case, the all-important subject matter is the psychosexual dynamics of men.

Chapter 1

That Which Is Learned

Train a child in the way he should go; and when he is old, he will not depart from it.

Proverbs 22:6

People are normally born with a capacity to feel pleasure when touched anywhere and with potential to develop sexual tensions. This is eventually coupled to a desire for stimulation and satiation. Neither men nor women are born with a specific preference for heterosexual, non-incestuous, private, emotionally involved, love-related, monogamous, children-desired sexual activity. In other words, all sexual preferences leading to satisfaction are learned. No matter what parents, clergymen or teachers may say, a child is actually a *very* pliable individual, devoid of any taboos, and unable to differentiate between what his elders consider "right" or "wrong."

Boys, like girls, learn about sex from parents, siblings, friends and all others with whom they come into contact. Some "lessons" are delivered deliberately, but most are conveyed without awareness, through identification and imitation. Some information is clear, concise and correct while other "facts" are muddled, confused and often grossly distorted. This information eventually involves ideas and feelings about oneself, members of the same sex and those of the opposite sex. It includes ideas involving rights, wrongs, good, and bad, and leads to combinations of spontaneous, free and even creative sexual behavior, as well as inhibitions and even sexual paralysis.

4

Sexual feelings start at birth and continue developing *long* before sexual union is actually possible. These feelings contain no limitations dictated by society, because in infancy conventional taboos have not yet been learned. Freud referred to these infantile sexual feelings, which are totally free of society-imposed restrictions, as "polymorphous perversus." In effect this means that very young children may enjoy oral, anal and any other bodily sensation in a sexual way—homosexually or heterosexually or autoerogenously—which as adults, they may come to consider "strange" or even "perverse." Residuals of these once acceptable infantile pleasures may result in attacks of self-hate, should they be remembered or felt as adults. A child may be innocently sexually excited by a parent or brother or sister, but for an adult, that's guilt-ridden incest. Harmless fantasies of sex with animals in childhood become bestiality when viewed in a grown-up context. A childishly naive attraction to a person of the same sex is interpreted as homosexuality later on in life.

Onset of puberty varies from climate to climate, from race to race and from person to person. Since patterns of sexual behavior and standards are learned, they too will vary from society to society. In one society incest and juvenile homosexuality are *natural* and *acceptable* and in others they're taboo. Some boys can eject semen as early as age nine, while others don't have ejaculatory ability until they are fourteen or fifteen—or older.

As men mature, it sometimes becomes difficult to sort out what society considers perverse, and even harder to define what constitutes acceptable masculinity. Feelings, ideas and thoughts that are considered perverse or unmanly are usually repressed. Repression leads to more confusion as well as to sexual problems of all kinds. Misinformation continues to abound, plaguing and confusing the adolescent just entering young adulthood. Today's so-called permissive society has provided both benefits and difficulties. One of these is the liberalization of puritanical restrictions on both a mental and physical level. This, if nothing else, has caused a partial reversal in the way the older generation sees the new one. For instance, not quite as many fathers still believe there's only "that kind of girl" to whom their sons can turn for quick satisfaction and a guaranteed "cure" for all sexual ignorance.

Certain ideas do linger, of course. One of these, for example, is the erroneous notion that a visit to a prostitute will solve all of a young man's sexual difficulties. The fact is that the average prostitute is just *not* capable of replacing his confusion and fear with confidence. On the contrary, she may succeed in making him feel even more inadequate. Prostitutes simply are not good teachers. They often lack real knowledge and sophistication. Few are sensitive, warm, accepting or the slightest bit altruistic. Many are stumbling by with misinformation and serious sexual, character and relating problems of their own. Others despise men. Most are basically hostile and in no way care to be teachers. The best sexual teachers in this or any other age are lovers who desire to give and take in an emotionally involved, sustained relationship.

Some women view men who have had many sexual escapades as guaranteed good lovers, but repeated sexual experience does *not* necessarily lead to sexual expertise. Sensitivity and caring are ingredients basic to the issue. Openness and a willingness to learn and a desire to please a loved one are much more important than quick conquests.

THE FAMILY INFLUENCE AND SEXUAL ATTITUDES

Parents aren't the only family members to exert an influence on boys. Siblings play important roles—sometimes positive, sometimes negative. A youngster is apt to get a good education in the psychological basics of female actions, reactions, whims and subtleties if he has a sister. That's even truer if he enjoys a *good* relationship with her. If his father holds the women of

6

the house in high esteem—and if the boy, too, enjoys high esteem—chances are better that the boy will mature with a generally high regard for women. In comparison, the youth who grows up without a sister has less contact and familiarity with females and is more susceptible to the age-old tales of the "good," "bad," "nice," "angelic" or "devilish" female. Because it's more difficult for him to enjoy a wide range of maturing experience that leads to worldliness, he tends to idealize women and think of them in terms of exotic fantasies.

A brother, on the other hand, may heighten competition and make it even more likely that the youngster will feel he has to live up to certain ideals of manhood and "macho" that often can't be matched—and ideally don't have to be. Of course, this all depends on the general tone and values in a household. Is the mood accepting or competitive? Naturalistic or perfectionistic? Broad-minded or narrow-minded?

I am often asked about the effects of sex education in school, especially in early schooling. Of course it can be helpful, especially as an adjunct to constructive information received at home. Much also depends on the benevolence, appropriateness, objectivity, sensitivity and expertise of the teacher. Children tend to do best with material appropriate to their level of intellectual and emotional development and sophistication. As in the family, the attitudes of the teacher regarding sex are of vital importance. A teacher who has not resolved his or her own sexual conflicts may well serve to confuse the students in this sensitive area, despite the attempt to deliver valid facts objectively. But even the best kinds of sex education delivered by the most knowledgeable and healthiest educators may increase a child's anxiety if it is at great variance with what he learns at home. It must be remembered that a child has learned the most vital and lifelong permeating information through his family, in the first few years of life, before he has commenced schooling. Indeed, most of his most important lessons, of which I will say more in the closing part of this chapter, are learned before he comprehends verbal language at all. Suffice it here to say that family influences in early life play a crucial role, but both proper and improper sex education in school may create disturbing emotional conflicts if it is at great variance with what has been learned at home.

As I've just indicated, children learn much earlier and also much more than that which is transmitted through spoken language. We might say that the music is much more important than the words. Indeed, children are exquisitely sensitive to household moods, which include the moods and feelings of all the people around them. They are superbly tuned in to tone of voice, the ways they are touched, small attentions and inattentions, the feelings of a mother during feeding and later on the feelings of family members at the dinner table, smells of all kinds (certain smells connote peace and comfort while others connote anxiety; I have a middle-aged patient who still feels anxious when she smells ammonia, remembering her mother's rough handling when changing her bed after wetting, in which the smell of urine was prevalent), discomforts and frustrations, and all kinds of emotional nuances. Nearly all workers in the field of human psychology and behavior agree that children are infinitely more sharply attuned than adults to *what is really felt* in a household (rather than to what is said). Perhaps we lose this extraordinary ability to perceive and to record what is going on in, about and to us as we get older due to the social and economic complications characteristic of adult life. Perhaps the fine instrument for perception of feelings we contain as children becomes blunted by the embroideries society imposes on our lives as adults. As I stated earlier, a child's perceptions include sexual information, thoughts, ideas, feelings and, eventually, values, desires and yearnings about himself, other people and the sexual area of human existence generally. But it must be remembered that the child does more than perceive. He also records! Without any attempt at memorizing, he records his learned feelings and intellectual information, and

8

usually records them in his unconscious for his entire lifetime. He is not aware that he is doing this, and later on in his life he may have no conscious awareness of the many feelings regarding sex which he has recorded, but his lack of awareness or consciousness does not diminish the power of that which he has recorded, and which through the years has become part and parcel of his sexual being as well as of his totality as a whole human being. I say *power* because these early recordings (stored memories, ideas, feelings) will largely dictate his sexual attitudes and actions as an adult. Psychoanalysts know full well that unconscious material constitutes the most powerful force in our lives; this is why analysis concerns itself with making that which is unconscious, conscious. Consciously knowing what motivates us is the only way we can really change, if we so desire. Some of us feel that the reason the child records his perceptions so effectively and with such proficient permanency is twofold. First, there is, as I indicated earlier, very little adult business to get in the way of his perceptions or the contents of his memory (compared to the event-laden memory of the adult). Second, the very young child is in his formative years, and perhaps that which is perceived in those years becomes part and parcel of the still developing, still evolving central nervous system (brain and spinal cord) and therefore becomes permanently contained in the very substance of the mind.

Unlike orthodox Freudians, I do not believe that sexual difficulties (*e.g.*, sexual frustration) produce neurosis, while relative sexual health provides a generally healthy life psychologically. I'm of the school that believes that one's sex life is largely a reflection and extension of one's whole psychological life, character and personality development. Therefore an individual who is relatively healthy emotionally will tend toward a constructive and fruitful sexual life. A man who suffers from personality and therefore relationship problems generally, will reflect these problems in the sexual area. This does not mitigate the importance of proper sex information and education, but it does put important

9

matters in the proper perspective. Therefore it is extremely important to realize that a great deal that occurs in early life that has little or no direct sexual connotation, but that affects us as total human beings generally, will eventually have the most profound effects on our sexual lives. Let me put it a little differently because this is so important. Our early development, in all areas, will play a paramount role in the kind of character structure we develop. That character structure (how we feel about ourselves and others generally—all areas, sex not excluded) will determine our behavior in all areas of living. That behavior will be reflected by our sexual attitudes and behavior. Therefore that which goes on in our childhood homes on a relatively non-sexual level will have an effect as profound, or even more profound, than that which is of an obviously sexual nature. Of course once our sexual lives are affected, this will in turn affect our personalities and lives generally, often making for a vicious cycle.

Obviously it is not within the scope of this book to describe or to explore early childhood development. Volumes have already been written on the subject. However, this concept is so important that in closing this chapter I would like to list several prime examples of relatively non-sexual early developments that strongly affect our sexual lives all of our lives. These developments are generally promoted, by examples, in members of the family with little or no awareness on their part.

1. How as children have we viewed, experienced and learned about the relationship of tenderness, intimacy, openness and love?

2. Was strength perceived and felt as being helpful and loving or manipulative, bullying and sadistic?

3. Were relationships in the family hostile, aggressive and competitive or trusting, helpful and cooperative?

4. Were compliance, conformity and self-effacement confused with femininity?

5. Were grandiosity, mastery and aloofness viewed as masculine?

6. Were self-control and a paucity of shows of emotion regarded as virtues?

7. Were feelings of family members repressed or expressed, especially strong and alive feelings of love and anger?

8. How did the family feel about their sons' special proclivities, and what were their expectations of sons?

9. How did the family feel about their daughters' special proclivities, and what were their expectations of daughters?

10. Was there respect or contempt for mother? for father?

Of course the key is *self-esteem*. How a man feels about himself will play the largest role in his sex life. Self-esteem must not be confused with synthetic vanity, sick narcissism and pompous grandiosity. Healthy self-esteem is always linked to healthy humility, a state in which an individual is well aware and accepting of both his assets and limitations. This enables him to enjoy the possibilities of mutual respect and of the give and take inherent in a satisfying sexual life. Self-esteem suffers terribly in a household in which prejudice of any kind exists. This includes prejudices against personal talents, proclivities and desires, as well as those against any member of the family for whatever reason. Self-esteem and esteem and respect for others, so necessary in a harmonious sexual relationship, suffer in a competitive, suspicious, paranoid household. Self-esteem suffers even more in a non-caring, ruthless household and still more in one which is stultifyingly overprotective. The two other most important ingredients to good sex are vitality and spontaneity. These suffer greatly in a household in which feelings are generally repressed.

A family in which children's natural tendencies and individuality are respected and encouraged, and in which all feelings are respected, cherished and expressed produces future adults who have a great share

11

of high self-esteem, vitality and spontaneity. This makes it possible to be an open person (open to one's own feelings and receptive to those of other people), to feel intimacy and to express tenderness through sex.

Chapter 2

Machismo!

> No healthy male is ever actually modest.
> No healthy male ever really thinks or
> talks of anything save himself. His con-
> versation is one endless boast—often cov-
> ert, but always undiluted. . . . Feminine
> strategy, in the duel of sex, consists al-
> most wholly of an adroit feeding of his
> vanity.
>
> —H. L. Mencken, *"The Smart Set,"*
> April 1919

Machismo!

What a word this is. Indefinable, yet defined in so
many ways: manliness, virility, masculinity, sexiness,
strength, control, power. There's nothing wrong with
any of the one-word qualities I listed above, just as
there's certainly nothing wrong with women who are
alluring, feminine, sensual, sexy and chic. It's the
excesses that cause the real problems, and in many
men machismo is one of the most crucial—and nearly
impenetrable—barriers standing in the way of a new
and healthier outlook.

Simple as it may seem, too many men think of
themselves as *men,* rather than as *human beings,* and
too often not as living, breathing, talented, vulnerable
and whole persons, but as mechanical, God-like yet
at the same time sad creatures. So many men feel this
way, and women (by virtue of their own cultural conditioning) have done little to make them feel otherwise. The inevitable result is a deeply ingrained
psychosexual value system that is extremely destruc-

tive. These men are unable to see beyond the confines of the male myth and become encumbered by impossible and confused notions about masculinity and femininity. Because their perceptions are diverted away from reality, many of their humanistic characteristics and assets are repressed to such an extent that vital caring emotions are numbed.

Many men are terrified that they will in some way exhibit womanly feelings. It is incredibly difficult for a man who questions his masculinity—a man who is confused about what truly defines gender—to display a touch of softness in the way he behaves.

If a man's feelings, especially empathetic, sympathetic, loving and generally softer ones, are deadened and repressed, his capacity for creativity and enjoyment is hampered too. Ultimately, everyone around him is victimized—his partner most of all. Repression of feelings always has reverberations in a man's sex life, where attempts to become an expert in sexual mechanics often take the place of what might otherwise be the lovemaking of a *whole human being*.

Where there is this repression women have one of the first of several opportunities to help their partners come to term with themselves. Women are generally freer than men to recognize and act out their total range of human sensitivities. Being human in all that *human* implies is basic to men and woman alike, but they don't always know this.

Unfortunately, in our power-conscious world, most men find it very painful to hear the truth when it runs counter to their own self-image, and that image, they are convinced, they must maintain. Many men fear psychological disintegration if they reveal themselves as being humanly vulnerable. So many men would profit enormously if their wives could slowly introduce them to the world of poetry, music, romance and yes, weeping and tears. A resurgence and evolvement of all that is human in the way of feelings must lead to a more interesting sexual life. Some men who are terribly frozen in their *macho mire* may need professional help in order to make progress in this all-important area. Unfortunately the very men who need help most usually refuse to consider professional counseling. To them, seeking psychological help demonstrates an inability to solve their own problems and implies weakness. This weakness means that some sort of "abnormality" exists, and the machismo male must believe above everything else that he is "normal."

Women in our culture do not have as much resistance to admitting either that they have emotional problems (they are usually more in touch with their feelings than men) or that they need help in solving those problems.

THE AURA OF MACHISMO

A large part of *being* in charge or radiating machismo lies in the *eyes* of the beholder. The image a man gives to the world very often depends on who is looking at him. "We are," as Jean-Paul Sartre, the French philosopher put it, "as others see us."

Some women are aroused by men in pinstriped business suits, while others respond to the sight of men in too-small T-shirts worn over rippling muscles. Tailored slacks and sports shirts unbuttoned to the navel may convey virility, and the sight of a man in uniform—any uniform—can be stimulating for some women.

Symbols play a role in the sexual lives of both sexes. Women may be preoccupied and more concerned than most men with the latest fashions, while men are more prone to concern and the quest for praise as regards symbols and issues involving their virility. Successful sexual performance provides one source of narcissistic reward, compliments on their physical appearance another. The message they transmit, "Look at me, I'm a Real Man," is often the basis of synthetic self-acceptance.

Very often a man tends to see and evaluate a woman

15

on the basis of *her looks;* a woman tends to see a man's looks for what they may represent. A dependent woman, for instance, may well be attracted to a man who she feels will be able to take care of her. This may or may not be related to physical characteristics. A dependent woman may mistake physical prowess for economic ability as well as for other capabilities related to taking care of her and her future family. Much depends on the kinds of symbols she has unconsciously ingested during her formative years. Since money plays a powerful role in our culture and very often unconsciously represents masculinity, many men adapt all kinds of affectations in order to seem more affluent than they are. Some men imitate movie actors, singers and popular heroes of the day in an effort to identify with women's current symbolic concept of *macho.* I remember a time when a whole population of men wore double-breasted suits and dangled cigarettes from their lips à la Humphrey Bogart. It's not so long since a huge number of men wore their hair like John Kennedy. Interestingly, these symbols may be quite effective, at least in initial contacts with some women.

Symbols play a large role in the lives of both sexes. Men, however, tend to be more simplistic, concrete and directly sexual in their interpretation of symbols. A man sees an exhibitionistic woman as a good sexual partner. A woman sees a "macho man" as a lover, provider, adviser, etc. Of course this isn't always the case; sometimes both men and women interpret symbols differently since symbol formation is a learned process.

May I also point out that men are great romantics, albeit on a secret, unconscious level. Therefore many men harbor during their entire lives images of themselves related to folk heroes of their childhood. These are often expressed symbolically through clothes worn, food eaten (steak is seen as a man's dish as a result of old Western movies), way of walking, style of speech and women to be seen with. I'll have more to say about hero identification in a little while.

MASCULINITY SYMBOLS: CULTURAL DIFFERENCES

Symbolism of any sort has roots in the very dawn of civilization. Much of it is related to male sexuality and cultural perceptions of masculinity. Crowns, medals and armor were only a *few* of the unmistakable trademarks of the male cult. In some societies, body paint indicated heroism or strength, and in others, more painful forms of bravado were prevalent.

To the inhabitants of Samoa, in the South Pacific, *tatooing* marked the moment of truth in a young man's life. Any man who underwent *that* type of ordeal didn't have to do much else to prove he was a man. Polynesian Islanders, who considered tatooing as artwork, a symbol of manliness and beauty, turned into living canvases. And if those tests weren't sufficient, there were always the incredibly awesome rituals of cicatrization that continue to this day. Any woman or man who has ever complained of an ingrown toenail or a splinter may consider what it must be like having cuts slashed on various parts of the body, then having the wounds *forced open* for lengthy periods of time to allow increased scar tissue to form! *National Geographic* magazine has reproduced countless photographs of men—and women—proudly wearing intricate designs which most of us would bury under make-up or rush to a plastic surgeon to cover. But then, how different is cicatrization from the pierced ears, "nose-job," muscle-building, hair-styling traumas touted in many of our more "civilized" societies?

For many years German men considered a dueling scar scratched prominently but neatly on a cheek the Aryan equivalent of a neon sign advertising masculinity. When a scar couldn't be won in actual combat, convenient duels were arranged. Not infrequently, a pocket knife used in the privacy of the bathroom was sufficient to produce an appropriate cut. The wound soon healed into a banner of manhood, broadcasting enough virility to win the respect of colleagues and to capture the hearts (and bodies) of female friends.

Hair, of course, has always enjoyed high symbolic significance, with various meanings in different times and places. Worn longish in one society, it indicated elegance, style, even artistic talent. Worn long elsewhere, it suggested dishevelment, rebellion, lack of couth and liberal political views. Short hair could mean neatness and toughness, failure to keep up with modern fashions, and a tendency toward a conservative political outlook, while baldness has often been considered a symbol of virility. This symbol may be somewhat related to fact, since pattern baldness may be influenced by testosterone, the male sex hormone.

Facial hair is another symbol, one particularly prevalent in our time, when many men have beards and mustaches. Whether or not those men have greater sexual competency is debatable, though a *beard,* according to some authorities, does seem to grow faster with increased sexual activity.

Hero Identification

Men do have other ways of finding their own version of macho. As I've indicated earlier, there's a *synthetic* kind of strength that evolves from identification with characters in movies (especially war films, cops-and-robbers and Westerns).

Films stressing war, gun battles and violence of any sort are the nether side of humanity and are antithetical to compassion, from which *real* strength springs. For men who are captivated by these movies and who derive a sense of manhood from them, the carry-over can be serious and destructive. All Marlon Brando had to do was make *one* film, *The Wild Ones,* to prompt many insecure boys in the country to hide behind the synthetic power shield of motorcycle jackets, hobnailed boots, black leather gloves and mirrored aviator sunglasses.

The inner motives that cause men to associate with strong characters in action films are related to those that compel them to get into fights. Worse yet, they are similar to those which allow them to go off to war with notions confusing masculinity, ruthlessness and the ability to murder without guilt. One of our culture's *great stimuli,* if we escalate sadism and the stimulation of violence to its ultimate degree, is war. Combat sexually stimulates many men, and for them, being part of the military—identifying with the strength of an army and its weaponry and having such unique masculine ties—often remains the highlight of their lives.

An overassociation with athletics, as strange and paradoxical as it may sound, can be an indication of emotional difficulty. The soldier and the athlete may be heroes, bold and capable of immense physical stamina, but a sports winner isn't *necessarily* sexually successful. Often, the man with the medals or laurel wreaths (or the man who associates with them vicariously) is an incompetent lover. He may be the symbolic prototype of virility and masculinity, but may lack the intensity of feeling, gentleness, imagination and sustained interest necessary to satisfy his partner *emotionally* as well as *physically*.

For any number of reasons, some women are *attracted* rather than repelled by these coldly efficient robots. They often misinterpret a withholding of human emotions as an indication of strength, manliness and dependability. If *she* also happens to have low self-esteem and *he* is particularly rough, mean and critical, she may even consider him wise. She will delegate to him her shreds of identity, and in glorifying him she will attempt to enhance her own ego.

Needless to say, all these premises are false, and terribly destructive to both partners.

19

SEXUAL PROWESS: MEN NEED A PASSING MARK

Most men (and their women) are adversely affected psychologically by the need to assert and maintain male pride at the highest possible level. As part of this need, men may subconsciously relate sexual prowess to athletics. From a *physical* viewpoint, they evaluate lovemaking in terms of performance and their ability to endure.

Many men not only have a need to prove themselves and to succeed, but also to be "the best" or *among* the very best. They aren't participants out to share an enjoyable experience; they're *performers,* forced to prove to themselves that they are very, very good. They want—they *need*—victory, gold stars, the genuine (not faked) applause and response of their audience of one. Their partners' orgasm is the sexual gold medal they are after and the key to their own sexual self-acceptance.

Male pride in sexual performance can be gargantuan. Few men want to be taken *anything less* than *seriously* in lovemaking; and nothing will bring down an erection quicker than a woman's joking or teasing during the sex act. Hurt pride can lead to *enormous* rage and, often, retaliation. In most cases, that counterattack is nothing much more than an injured expression or a sharp word or two, though some men may resort to real violence.

Chapter 3

Men's Fears

> The mind is its own place, and in itself
> Can make a heaven of Hell, a hell of
> Heaven.
> —John Milton, *Paradise Lost*

Most men can admit to certain realistic fears—the depressed state of the economy, paying the rent, an unhappy job situation or even the threat of a world war—but will have great difficulty conceding that they are frightened of being sexual creatures.

I need hardly say that most men want to be known as sexual creatures. The conflict arises because they are embarrassed by their own sexuality and terrified of their own performance standards. While they are very much interested in being considered sexually exciting by women, they are, at the same time, worried about what will be expected of them. Men who are particularly self-effacing, compliant and conforming will be especially embarrassed by any evidence of their own sexuality—evidence that they *are*, indeed, sexual creatures—just as they would be by indications of any appetite of a strong nature.

Most men are neither as sexually liberated nor as uninhibited as they imagine themselves to be. Most men still find that buying a sex magazine is *not* as simple a matter as buying *Reader's Digest* or the daily newspaper. The revised openness and liberalized public attitude toward sex in recent years has made it *easier*, but not *easy*. For a man to purchase a sex-oriented publication, he has to *risk* the unwritten but ominous threat that other people will consider him *incapable* of finding a woman to fill his sexual needs. Or that they will assume he is unable to be fully satisfied with his current sexual relationships. A sex magazine means that he *must* be frustrated; that he *must* be using the pictures to help him masturbate; that he is a sexual creature. And *if* he's a sexual creature, he's also unavoidably susceptible to urges, emotions and drives *beyond his control* that offer a challenge to his strength and dominance.

It would be convenient to conclude that these were the only pertinent illustrations, but as many women already know, men exhibit *just as many* (and similar) fears if forced by circumstances to go to the corner drugstore for contraceptives or for a package of sanitary napkins for their wives.

Go into any movie theater screening pornographic films and note not only the interesting age variety in the audience but, what is even more fascinating, that the customers hardly look at each other, as if adhering to a strict, secret code stipulating, "If *you* don't see *me*, and *I* don't see *you*, then neither of us will know the the other was here." In other words, then *no one* will know that any of the men at the performances are sexual creatures with sexual curiosities and sexual desires. One major reason men prefer films to live sex shows is because the movies are shown in a *dark* theater. At a live show a man often worries that the spotlight may fall upon *his* head, singling *him* out to one and all. The same fears involved in the purchase of a sex magazine come into play here. Will "people" think he's lonely and frustrated? Will they think this is a kind of masturbatory experience, relegating him to adolescent level, although he's a fully grown adult? More pertinently, will people see him as a sexual entity, a fear particularly nerve-racking to a self-effacing man who doesn't want to be seen as too much of an individual of human substance and weight in any area.

"LOVE" IS HARD TO SAY

Taking all of this one step further, there's an even *more* intense, *more* prevalent fear: *expressing* (*revealing* may be a better word) *emotions.*

It is extremely demanding for many a man to tell a woman, "I love you." Saying these words implies a commitment, and most often an exclusive relationship. This is true not only for bachelors who are afraid deeper involvement may lead to marriage (and entrapment if not downright inundation); it plagues the married as well. Most *women* have a great need to hear those words, and men who realize this—many responsible men *do*—are still hesitant to say them. They are inhibited to the point of paralysis. For the woman, "I love you" is reassurance of her loveability and sometimes dilutes feelings of inadequacy, self-doubt and self-contempt. Particularly dependent women, who feel their only earthly salvation can be found in a perfect love, grab at the words like drowning swimmers. Sometimes, of course, the words are as solid as land; sometimes they are as meaningless and as vacuous as clouds.

Dependent *men* like to hear the words just as much as their female partners, but that doesn't mean they find it any easier to say them. Most women simply don't have the same emotional blocks.

Many relatively well-adjusted women also want to hear an "I love you" now and then because it *does* have an extra-special meaning. Delivered by her lover, it means: (1) she exists as a person; (2) she is a woman and he accepts her femininity; (3) she is desirable, attractive sexually, intellectually and in countless other ways; (4) he is interested in who she really is; (5) he accepts her human liabilities as well as her human assets; (6) theirs is an exclusive relationship, not shared in quality and intensity of feelings by anyone else; (7) she isn't alone, but accompanied by a man who cares as much about her well-being as about his own; (8) their relationship is one of mutual interest and trust; and (9) she is of primary importance to him and he doesn't take her for granted. If a woman has to *ask,* insist or beg a man to tell her he loves her, symbolic significance is weakened. Spontaneity and warmth evaporate, leaving behind a residue of contrivance and frustration.

The question then arises, if men also like to hear the words, and if they have the emotional ties that actually make it valid for both partners to say them, what is the difficulty all about?

Ned was like so many men when he said to me, "I love Jill, but it's hard to tell her that. I don't know why, except that it sounds foolish. I get a knot in my stomach when I think of opening up and showing that I'm vulnerable. I don't want to seem that vulnerable, *even to myself.* If you show emotion, you're not being rational, in command."

In one important respect, Ned was very fortunate. At least he had some insight. Other men, including married ones, have other reasons for shying away from "I love you." For some, the expression is *too committal* and for others, precisely the opposite is true. They've said it *so many* times to *so many* women that it's lost all meaning. Men who have not made an adequate break with their mothers feel the words are disloyal, even unfaithful to her. Others withhold them as revenge and as a special way of imparting hostility to a partner.

Tragically, if a man is convinced a display of emotions *isn't* masculine, he won't use the words "I love you" during lovemaking, the *one occasion* when their use is most appropriate. Refraining from showing feelings, he upsets his partner and disrupts the love and sexual mood they share. Revealing feelings, however, can depress him and may even lead to a period of temporary impotence. He is caught, trapped, closed in on all sides by a situation that imperils his feeling of macho no matter *which* course he eventually takes. Without genuine emotion, even minor physical signs of affection such as kissing are bound to be mechanical.

Some men who are afraid to exhibit feelings resort to teasing because it serves as a barrier and false front, which helps them avoid the need to reveal true emotions. Through the use of teasing, men can displace affection as well as hostility. Teenage boys rely on this tactic with friends they like, just as adult men too often utilize it to establish contact with children.

REJECTION

The dread of rejection, sexually, socially and professionally, is an integral part of the fear mechanism that leads many adult men to seek out women, friends and jobs they know are inappropriate for them in one way or another. A man sometimes feels that he runs *fewer risks* of being told no by a less attractive, less intelligent, less charming woman. He runs *fewer risks* of being turned down for a job that demands less experience, education and talent and pays less than for one that requires maximum expertise and background. This seemingly practical, though pathetic approach to living often starts at a relatively early age. Of course poor self-esteem has many roots and most of them are related to what goes on in early family life. But traumatic experiences with girls and young women during the years of development have considerable effect on an already weakened structure. Nothing will do more to shake a young man's confidence and self-esteem than to be told by the girl he has chosen that she *won't* accompany him to the spring prom. If he's resilient enough he'll try again with the same young woman or with another he finds nearly as captivating. Most boys can't handle too much rejection beyond that point, so "second best" or even no one *at all* becomes the alternative. Before long, there's a very real chance that "first choices" (be they with a potential date, a particular club, team or fraternity, course of study, college or career) will be avoided *completely*. By eliminating even the slightest possibility of rejection, an old truism is flipped in reverse: "If you don't ever ask, you'll never be told no."

All of this accounts in part for the sense of resignation a large segment of the male population seems to harbor. Limiting and killing off real desires in order to avoid disappointment and frustration provides a kind of shaky and sad protective device. But of course it also leads to increased *inner* deadness and loss of interest—and this may include sexual interest.

Tagging along into manhood, this sense of "I'm number two" undermines the basic foundation so vital to every individual's stability. It is an important theme, which will appear in several forms in our upcoming discussions.

Chapter 4

Dependency

Who ran to help me when I fell,
And would some pretty story tell,
Or kiss the place to make it well?
My mother.
—Ann Taylor, "My Mother"

Undeniably, most men are *very* dependent on women. This is true sexually, in family life, in business and in nearly all areas of human existence. And, of course, dependency, as it is defined by men, connotes weakness. Interdependency—that is, dependency on one another—is characteristic of human existence and comprises what we've come to view as society in all of its ramifications.

There are people who are morbidly and chronically overdependent and who feel an almost complete lack of identity unless they are firmly attached (emotionally) to another human being. But this sick condition must not be confused with normal human dependency. Most men, however, equate nearly any kind of dependency with weakness, and this has been characteristic of men through the ages. While there may have been special need in many instances for independence and dependence on one's self, some of these historical needs have become grossly exaggerated idealizations. For example, in our own country, which prides itself on the pioneering spirit, where "moving West" demanded that men be not only courageous and strong, but able to survive alone in the wilderness, a dependent male was the wrong type of person in the wrong place at the wrong time.

27

Most people all over the world would still find it difficult to imagine their favorite heroes laying down gun or sword long enough to talk tenderly about mother or any other woman, be it wife, girlfriend, or mere acquaintance.

Here in the United States, for instance, rugged plainsmen and Indian fighters just didn't go around discussing mama. Mothers were, and are, the ultimate dependency figures, born and bred to be responsible for children. It is true that after a certain age (differing from one individual to another), men must escape their female caretakers and fend for themselves emotionally and physically. Breaking away from Mama, as a matter of fact, remains one of the most trying transitions faced by men (though most *do* transfer dependence to another woman). Some men are fortunate in having mothers who recognize the necessity of this psychological rite of passage and who handle the shift with delicacy, understanding and love. Others, fearful that the step means giving up a son, hold on and thwart the boy, creating guilt as well as unhappiness.

In more sophisticated societies for example (Paris, at the turn of the century), there was allowance for strong females who might be caring for men engaged in more genteel and artistic pursuits. (This also occurs when men are engaged in long training programs involving various professions. A number of my classmates in medical school were *extremely* dependent on wives who earned an income, paid the bills and managed the household. But dependency for most men is often impossible to admit or to accept even in cases where it leads to constructive purpose for both parties. Dependency means not only weakness but helplessness, and men fear if they are needy they will once again become children. This fear often results in a flight away from the woman on whom they are actually dependent, who is unconsciously perceived as mother.

There certainly are many men today who have been personally tested by intense familial, communal and natural exigencies that made it necessary for them to call on every last bit of their own reserve to withstand a loss of freedom, sanity or even life. A man strong enough to survive the degradation of a concentration camp or life in a run-down ghetto, the destabilizing effect of parents killed while he was young, the sickening rejection of racial or ethnic prejudice, or the financial battering of a natural disaster or business loss, has been through the fire and *usually* knows what strength and dependency are all about. Yet even these men, having received a first-hand feel of their own strength, as well as the necessity for depending on others to survive, are often no more prone to accept *their own* dependency than any other man. Some, having "proven themselves," are even *more reluctant* to dispel the manly image. Some men, even if they want to let loose, can't because of the high expectations of those who have looked to them for guidance and support.

The problem of dependency is a twofold one. There is the aspect already discussed, of the reluctance of men to admit needs and to depend on others; but there is another aspect: their unwillingness to allow others to depend on them, and their inability to cope with the needs of others.

"They depend on me for everything," said one of my patients, referring to his family. "For their home, for their clothes, their food, their guidance . . . everything. Sometimes I feel I can't handle it." This man had a valid point; his family *had* seemingly abdicated their own responsibilities in favor of allowing him to handle them. However, it was not the practical problems that he was really objecting to. First of all, he wanted to be considered not as a robot who existed for their benefit, but as a human being who had moments when he, too, needed comfort and consolation; moments when he did not want to be the wise, all-deciding patriarch. This is understandable. But, as we talked, it was apparent that his underlying dissatisfaction lay with the emotional dependence his family imposed upon him. His real objection was not that he supported his family and that they expected him to support them, but that this material dependency was a cover-up

29

for emotional needs that he was neither equipped, nor wanted to handle.

There is a great deal of role playing that people do in their adult years. At various times every man feels the need to be a child, to be—though usually momentarily—in a dependent situation. If he is sick, he will want to be mothered, or if he is feeling particularly vulnerable, to rest his head against a woman's breasts. And then, there are the moments when he must be in the position of authority, when he has to play father. But many men are not the "fathering" type. Many are more comfortable playing "child." Sometimes the individual who is predominantly the "father," projecting the image of the strong authoritarian, is actually manipulative and, in some respects, sadistic. Frequently this kind of man may be repressing an enormous amount of dependency by throwing up an unusually forceful front. A similar stratagem is used by men who feel particularly fragile and inadequate and who overcompensate and cover up by acting arrogantly. The degree of arrogance is directly proportionate to the amount of underlying fear and feelings of fragility.

More often than not, the arrogant and "overly strong father" personality camouflages the frightened man attempting to convince the outside world, and himself, that he is as strong internally as the image he projects.

Though it may shatter a few women's illusions, nearly *every* man needs reassurance at one time or another. Some need it almost every single day. There are many for whom no amount of bolstering is *too much,* and yet it must be done in a quiet, loving, intelligent, honest way. Often it doesn't take much to shatter a man's shaky self-esteem. So many men must be *assured* and *reassured* (and *reassured* again if necessary) that they are good, that they are doing the right thing, and that they are loved, respected and wanted.

Many single women feel that they are victims of a man's whims. They can't ever take the initiative and ask a man for a date. Yet many women don't seem to comprehend the fear, the near terror of young men as they try to get up the nerve to ask a classmate to the movies or to the local ice-cream parlor for a soda and hamburger. This difficulty can be carried on from adolescence, through the teens, into adulthood and as long as a new and unknown challenge presents itself. *No male wants to be rejected,* no matter what the situation, and this holds just as true for job-hunting as it does for dating.

Although particularly dependent men appreciate an assertive woman because they *can* lean on her, they may also feel that this same dependency threatens their masculinity. Paradoxically many men conclude that a woman who is *not* taking the initiative (in bed, for instance) is somehow rejecting them, while a woman who *is* taking the initiative is effecting a challenge to their manhood. As Victorian as it all may appear, especially in this age of the feminist movement, many men are extremely threatened by assertive, let alone by so-called aggressive women.

People aren't like magnets. Opposites don't attract each other, nor repel one another. I've known several instances where two extremely dependent individuals didn't discover until they were married that the wife was looking for "Daddy" and the husband for "Mommy." When they realized neither could provide the other with this deep psychological need, they both felt *enormously* shaken. One woman in particular came to see me complaining that she had a "weak" husband. She wasn't the overbearing type, but actually rather dependent and consequently disappointed, not in her husband as much as in *herself.* Since she always waited for her partner to take the responsibility, *nobody made any decisions.* The husband wanted to be the "son," and the woman, the "daughter." I referred both of them to therapists to help them overcome their considerable morbid dependency.

Anyone who thinks that men *don't* search for Mama in the women they marry need only look at some statistics. Surveys indicate that *more than twice* the number of men who married women resembling their real mothers sustained marriage as compared to those who married women who bore no resemblance.

The emotional carry-over is interesting. Any woman who has shared a relationship with a man (living together, whether or not married) may recall from personal experience that Mama *can't* get sick! Most men are particularly testy and go through great difficulties if their partner becomes incapacitated in any way. That goes for a common cold, menses, and pregnancy, as well as for more serious problems with long range, lasting effects. In fact, harsh as it sounds, a man can more readily accept his partner's being *crippled* in a car accident than he can her staying in bed with sneezing, coughing and a runny nose.

This is in keeping with male dependency needs and poor frustration tolerance. If his partner is bedridden, he'll have to make breakfast himself. He'll also probably have to comfort *her* after *he* has had a hard, busy session in the office, instead of having her greet him at the door with a warm welcome (even if she's arrived only minutes before him from her job). Sexually, he's on his own, too, and very often he's better off masturbating than allowing that addition tension to pressure him further.

No matter how much men try to remain independent, those who are heterosexual are still dependent on women for *love, sex* and *companionship*. Any man who hasn't made a relatively clean break with his real mother inevitably faces an even more difficult inner conflict. Some resort to hypersexuality (or at least talk of incredible sexuality and conquests) while some others turn to the macho world of athletic and military prowess, where there is the potential—if they want to move in that direction—for substituting other outlets for those normally used to release more gentle emotional energies. Men more certain of themselves are usually less drawn to "masculine" activities and can better devote themselves to providing women with warmth, understanding and genuine affection.

Conflicts involving dependency and independency as well as confusions regarding masculinity are apparent at a relatively early age. The sexual fantasies of *most young boys* already suggest protecting Mama, of being super-masculine. They may see themselves with sword (here a tool of *real aggression,* and sometimes also a phallic symbol) in hand, conquering the dragon. As these fantasies progress over the years, the dreams of glory stimulate sexuality in a masculine way.

For some men, aggression translates into sadism, generally directed toward women. Sadistic aggression most often is utilized to alleviate deadness, though I must say that it is not necessarily a masculine trait at all, nor is it always manifested sexually or physically. In fact, it *frequently* involves the manipulation of others. It is via the infliction of pain in others that some persons discover that they themselves are stimulated. If we assume that aggression is a form of sadism through the use of a vicarious experience, then it is easy to understand the motivations of a man who *insists* that his partner achieve an intense orgasm. Just the fact that he is insisting removes the possibility that he is concerned solely with his partner's pleasure. Instead, his goal is to enhance his own sense of masculinity and, in some cases, to feel a—sadistic, if you will—sense of mastery.

There's often a confusion between feelings of love and dependency. Many men think they're merely dependent upon a particular woman rather than deeply in love with her, while others have the opposite conviction. The case of the medical students and working wives that I cited earlier in this chapter serves as an example. Greg, an easterner newly enrolled in a Midwestern medical school, believed, or deluded himself into believing, that he wanted to marry Francine purely out of a deep and abiding love. Sadly, it developed, as it often does, that Greg had married Francine to get a partner he could depend on physically, emotionally and economically, while he struggled through school. When he graduated and started to build a practice and a bank account, he found that he didn't *truly* love her, even though she had shared all those hard years with him. Love involves mutual caring and he really didn't care for her. She was little more than an emotional and economic crutch he had leaned upon during a trying period, and the marriage eventually ended in divorce, and also in a state of considerable hatred. When feelings of dependency are despised, the self-hate engendered is often projected to the very person whom one depends on.

Chapter 5

Detachment: Fears of Intimacy and Involvement

> It is when we try to grapple with another
> man's intimate need that we perceive how
> incomprehensible, wavering, and misty
> are beings that share with us the sight of
> the stars and the warmth of the sun.
> —Joseph Conrad, *Lord Jim*

A great many men in our society are detached. In fact, the seeking of freedom from emotional involvement or commitment as a way of coping with anxiety and creating a cloak of self-protection is understandably quite appealing.

The real difficulty with detachment is that it is not genuine, uncomplicated freedom, but a *compulsive* need for freedom that is seldom used for constructive purposes. Men who fall into this category are afraid of any contractual agreement and approach most issues from a negative, rather than positive, point of view. Terrified of becoming engulfed, detached men make a fetish of freedom. In avoiding commitment they become "You mind *your* own business," "I'll mind *my* own business" people. Ask them, "What do you think of this food?" and they won't answer "It's good," but, "It's not bad." Ask them, "Do you want to go to a show two weeks from now?" and they'll reply, "Maybe." Even that commitment is too much for them.

As indicated earlier, all of us need people, and this need establishes a difficult conflict for men who prefer to remain independent. On the one hand, they are inclined strongly to move *away* from other men and women, yet on the other hand, they are drawn to others for all reasons inherent in being human. Many men, therefore, involve themselves in relationships that they never quite allow to arrive at full fruition. Since it's not unusual for a loss of freedom in these men to provoke severe anxiety, quite a few would-be bridegrooms succumb to panic on the eve of their marriages. Once they are wed, they have decided, they will have become irrevocably trapped and stripped of their own identity.

Of course since all of this can be terribly injurious and eroding to a relationship in general terms, it usually also provides sexual difficulties. Sexual repercussions such as impotence may occur in cases where the man—and this is without any actual or implied homosexuality playing a role—even finds it threatening to sexually penetrate a woman because of the closeness and attachment the act symbolizes to him.

Other men who suffer from the same sort of psychological restraints find that they *can* get an erection, but can't ejaculate. For them, ejaculation subconsciously represents a form of giving, a consummation and, worst of all, a further evidence of commitment. Transferring semen would also represent an investment as well as concrete potential for creating a child. Of course a child means even further involvement and commitment.

Added to all of this is the continuing, inescapable fact that for women—the feminist movement notwithstanding—marriage remains a sign of enhanced prestige in the community. Someday it may be different, but it holds true for the time being. Further, most of our nation and its various institutions are attuned to accepting a woman *with a man,* rather than alone. Since most women have unfortunately been raised with the notion that they themselves are in large part defined by marriage and the man they marry, their pride is enhanced by wedlock. The same cannot be said for men.

If a man gets married, he usually does not in his

own mind enhance his prestige to any large degree. He certainly will no longer be the town bon vivant, the free bachelor able to win the hearts and sexual charms of many women. Too often, for him (and for many of his male friends), he is settling down to engulfment and, more tragically, to old age. There won't be any more sowing of any wild oats. And it doesn't really matter whether or not he did sow before marriage. Since he has agreed not to do it from his wedding day on, he is giving something up. He is, in short, surrendering a freedom of action.

Once a man is married, he must aggressively pursue a course almost directly in contrast to the one he followed when single. In place of freedom, he is now responsible for earning all, or a significant part of, the family income. Even with the shifting of contemporary mores, it's not very likely the average man will sit home and care for the baby while his wife spends the day at work. In common situations such as these, men are easily threatened, especially if they are basically keyed to a sense of personal inadequacy.

As we've seen, the very same men who are making every effort to be independent are generally very dependent, too. A large part of the attraction to a particular woman lies in the man's desire to be able to depend on *her*. As indicated earlier, dependency up to a point is a normal reality. They will, after all, depend on each other for sex, a socioeconomic balance in their household and companionship. Still, a woman can deal with those feelings far more easily than a man, for whom dependency is automatically equated with weakness.

If a man has an unusually strong unconscious need to be independent and also dependent and has stirred up *both* feelings of dependency and independency, he undergoes a conflict that creates within him enormous feelings of anxiety, fear, distrust, paranoia and even hostility toward his wife. It is this conflict that is often responsible for the beginnings of deterioration in a relationship almost immediately after the contract is signed (or the vows taken). Unless there is an accommodation to this position or some outside help is sought, many such marital partnerships can, and do, end before their first anniversary arrives.

In this situation a man rarely mentions the part played by his fears of engulfment, nor does he discuss the wealth of injunctions that hit him when he sealed the marital pact: he *should not* be interested in other women; he *should not* be tempted to stray; he *should not* ever be weak; he *should not* ever be irresponsible, etc. Up to the point of commitment, unfortunately, he had a freedom of choice he now must give up.

For many men, therefore, a logical way to avoid all disturbing problems like these is to avoid involvement altogether. The burden then shifts to the woman, who must be assertive and soothing enough to bring the man to the point of commitment. Unless she is, the man frightened of intimacy and involvement will flee.

Frequently, communication is a means of solving some of these particular conflicts, but here again, not every man (or woman) knows *how* to communicate. When a woman's dependency needs come into collision with a man's need for freedom, communication is mandatory. Much then depends on the couple's willingness to open themselves up to one another. A detached man, however, does not communicate very well. When he's angry, there's much less of a tendency for him to explain his anger than there is for him to sulk. Explaining his anger, after all, is a positive move forward that clearly represents involvement. Sulking, in contrast, represents withdrawal—and that in itself represents a form of freedom and lack of involvement.

Chapter 6

Women

For the study of the good and bad in
    women,
Two women are a needless expense.
            —Ambrose Bierce, *Epigrams*

The subject of this chapter might seem surprising, but if women are to *really* understand men, then it is important that they understand something of men's perceptions about women.

How many of us have heard male friends mutter the mournful lament, "I don't understand women sometimes"? It's a fairly popular refrain. Yet, as with so many other expressions, the roots of the complaint merit closer inspection. Most men have always assumed that women are *completely* different from them, and because of that have regarded them as strange creatures whose minds and motivations must inevitably remain a mystery.

As in all areas and subjects lacking understanding, women were usually viewed in different ways by different cultures. To some, they were powerful and mysterious beyond *all* comprehension. We have ample evidence from historians and archeologists of the large and varied assortment of goddesses created and revered by both primitive and civilized societies. A woman's unique ability to mother a child (for quite a while men didn't recognize the connection between intercourse and procreation) earned her idolization and fear; her ability to seduce men with the bait of desire earned her an equal amount of suspicion. On the one hand she was the goddess of love, beauty and fertility, and on the other the siren of mythology—part woman, part bird—whose seductive songs lured sailors to watery graves.

Woman was strong and "dangerous" in other ways, too. She tended to live longer, to ward off disease better than men and to recover more quickly when illness or injury did take hold. But she also was *weak*, unable in most instances to join in battle against an enemy or to hunt for the game that would put food on the fire. When she did become pregnant, she was of little practical help and was also believed to be hampered, limited and particularly dependent when menstruating. Just picture early man faced with this incredible, inexplicable monthly event. What else could it be but evidence that evil spirits were at work and in control? Men had to watch out for women. They couldn't be trusted.

Today, the majority of men still shy away from sexual relations during a woman's menstrual cycle, but for other reasons. Some are repelled by the appearance and thought of sex during this time, while others rely on the more traditional appraisal that women are "unclean" during menstruation. Still others are more graphic and terrified in their reluctance. They fear that intercourse will result in castration. In some rare cases it may be unconscious dread of "vagina dentata," the toothed vagina.* Any vaginal blood conjures up horrifying thoughts of mutilated penises. Some psychiatrists feel that this extreme is usually found in men who have been symbolically castrated by their parents, especially by mother. These are men whose self-esteem was crushed in early childhood and who may have additional problems with their own psychological identities.

From a non-psychological standpoint, the lack of attraction to menstruation may be understandable on an esthetic level. But it is also interesting to note that some men see it as particularly feminine and stimulat-

---

* Men troubled by this problem experience dreams in which women's vaginas—usually that of their dream partner—actually have teeth.

ing and still others use it as an adjunct to fantasies in which they brutalize their lovers.

Vaginal odors, bowel noises, belching and other bodily evidence of human physiology also enter the picture here. It goes without saying that proper and regular hygiene is essential to sexual allure, though the *most thorough attention* (and even the added inducement of perfumes) sometimes has limited effect. Some men accept smells and sounds when they are convinced that every effort was made to avoid them. Some cannot. There are those who are unable to cope with reality, any evidence of a woman's physiological existence destroys the idealized illusion. Many women have been asking for—demanding—equality, yet their husbands or lovers continue to idealize them as if they were modern descendants of ancient goddesses.

Morris spent the forty-one years of his marriage giving his wife, Janet, all the love and affection he could muster. She adored him, except for one particular complaint. "I can't *walk to the bathroom* in the morning without having every hair in place."

Morris indisputably had a slight touch of the idealization syndrome. For many men, their repulsion to such natural functions as feminine odors and human bodily sounds is in *direct proportion* to their idealization of women. The more immature a man is, the more he tends to put them on a pedestal where they can stand above all mortal frailties and shortcomings, then the more enraged and revolted he becomes at anything that reminds him in the slightest way that they're *just as human* and prone to mortal limitations as anyone else after all.

One Step Backward, Two Steps Ahead

The first thing any man who really *wants* to understand women must do is to admit to himself seriously that there really are gaps in his understanding. Only then can he come to grips with any stored up fear and hostility. Despite boasts to the contrary, however, not too many men are willing to go that far. Many even unintentionally confuse affection and attraction with understanding. Men's prefabricated knowledge about women is usually riddled with infantile and adolescent fears, fantasies, prejudices and exaggerations. Surely one of the most simplistic of these masculine misconceptions is that *all women* are alike. Men will readily admit that they are attracted to certain, specific, well-defined "types" of women, but then refuse to see them as individuals.

While male prejudice against women—like female prejudice against men—can have disastrous consequences, women are *generally more mature* in seeking to learn what they can about men. Male pride and lack of maturity mitigate against reverse attempts.

We know that many men have an intense drive for what they see as masculine characteristics of strength, emotional control, courage, complete absence of helplessness, logic, constant youth, physical prowess, sexual potency and glory through competition and aggression. They have problems accepting the notion that, if they are strong, women *aren't* necessarily weak; if they are in control of their emotions, then women may be in control of theirs, too. (Of course being "in control of emotions" is a dubious asset, indeed. It frequently leads the "controller" to lose touch with his real feelings. It is difficult, if not impossible, to relate to one's self and to others if our emotions are utterly repressed or deadened.)

It isn't easy for men to understand that there's *nothing exclusively masculine or feminine* about depression, cowardice, envy, jealousy or love; or about sexual interest, artistic talent or involvement with children; or about shyness, greed, generosity, and hundreds of other traits. Young boys, raised to be "men" and not "sissies," are told that associating with girls *isn't masculine*. Giving that advice is the same as cutting wires on a telephone line; it creates a large and immediate gap in communication and understanding. Maturity brings little impetus for change, and there's even a regression in later life when husbands (and wives) have only friends of their own sex in order to avoid the hint or threat of any non-platonic heterosexual relationships.

Women *can help* their partners understand them better, but the effort requires a great deal of patience and compassion. For example, in the sexual area, unless women tell them, many men find it difficult to realize that unlike themselves, women sometimes find sex satisfying or enjoyable without orgasm. Men have to set aside male pride before they can possibly realize that women *are* capable of understanding and sharing business, checking accounts, politics, plumbing, electricity, football and all the other interests and provinces so many men consider *exclusively* theirs. Just as parents play an enormous role in shaping a young boy's feelings of humanity and masculinity, they can widen his understanding of girls and the women they will eventually become.

As outdated as it may seem, categorizing women as either "angels" or "devils," a problem that troubled the ancients, still persists today. In centuries past, for instance, women were often kept virginal to prevent them from becoming pregnant before marriage. Since line of descent (or succession) was through the male, it was mandatory to know who the father was. Today, despite social change and the advent of effective birth control measures, which eliminate that rationale for virginity, the double standard persists.

Men, who are *always* in search of *some* form of sexual satisfaction, often see women as having relatively little sexual appetite or need. But at the same time many young men believe that loss of virginity is *guaranteed* to radicalize a girl from a sweet, innocent, harmless, angelic creature into a wild, worldly, dangerous, devilish female . . . even a potential "whore." To cover the various situations, people long ago devised a simple, incredibly unjust rating system. There were the "good" girls, who were said to "go out on a date, go home, and go to bed"; the "nice" girls, who could be counted on to "go out, go to bed with the one man in

43

their lives and go home"; and the "bad" girls, who were ready to go to bed regardless of who their partners were.

In the midst of this sexual evolution, men developed an intensified longing for a woman who could express herself sexually, but who *also* was inhibited enough that she wouldn't run the risk of becoming promiscuous. For many of these men, the "good" women were *too* good, the "bad" women *too* bad and the whole thing thoroughly confusing.

Men want women to be sexually available to them. They also want women to be sexually competent— only, by the way, in *their* beds—but they are terrified of women who openly express their own sexual desires and needs.

If a woman enjoys sex and accepts her enjoyment without hesitation, some insecure men often translate this to mean that a woman is insatiable and that she will seek fulfillment anytime, anyplace. Because some men are not as keyed in to sex with particular partners and find it easier to have sex with women with whom they are not emotionally involved, they assume that, like them, women will have sex with a multiplicity of partners, given the opportunities.

There is even the extraordinarily erroneous idea prevalent among certain men that the woman who enjoys sex will eventually become a prostitute. These men don't realize that many prostitutes are neither heterosexual nor working for anything but money. A considerable percentage of prostitutes are homosexual. Prostitution is a job . . . and a very demanding one. Also, prostitutes rarely have orgasms with "Johns," and when they do, the release can be a tiring nuisance, making it more difficult to accommodate quite as many clients. To ensure that their partners don't take this "satanic" path, many men will pursue and marry women who seem (or who are) sexually repressed, believing that they are more likely to be "faithful."

Just the physiological fact that a woman can recycle for renewed intercourse a lot quicker (and thus more often) than a man is a harmless reality that many men transform into a fearsome threat. "I have to wait until I get an erection but all *she* has to do is spread her legs and she's ready for it again and again!"

THE DOUBLE STANDARD

.A sexual double standard still exists. It is a by-product of the unconscious fear that women will discover their superior sexual endurance and ability, and once they do, will use it against men to diminish them.

One way we can see this double standard at work is in the way men publicly promote the attractiveness of their women. Most males *want* their partners to be attractive—feminine as well as sensual—because the more *other men* covet a man's partner, the prouder and more masculine he will feel. But many *women* enjoy playing the "tease game." In that popular pastime, they test their allure by wearing clothes keyed to catch the eyes of men, then turn around and act insulted or angry when the sought-after look of appreciation and interest is obtained.

Exactly what constitutes alluring clothes depends very much on the particular society involved, just as it does in determining what portions of the anatomy are especially arousing. Because breasts and buttocks usually represent the greatest apparent differences between the sexes, they are the characteristics most emphasized by women and noticed by men. In certain times and places, large breasts have been considered the ultimate and determinative signs of feminine sexuality, but even where they are downplayed, many men remain attracted to them for the comfort and warmth they symbolize as well as for the physical pleasure they promise. Breasts, after all, are easily associated with mother's milk and her caring and kindness.

The man who encourages his partner to flaunt her femininity to bolster his own sense of machismo is looking for trouble and sending out a mixed-up message: "Look, but *don't* look" at her beautiful face, her round, firm breasts, her shapely legs, those lovely eyes, the stylish way she sits down or stands up. He loves the risks but is petrified by the consequences. If the tease is successful, he can easily erupt into jealousy the moment another man *does* look with anything more than a passing glance.

Bill, a man in his thirties, got the biggest thrill escorting his much younger, sexy dates to restaurants and parties. The tighter their sweaters, the lower-cut their dresses, the slinker their gowns, the prouder he was. He was always intent on gauging the reactions of the other men in the room. His routine had become compulsive: he'd glance away from his date or his plate to see which men—and how many—were giving her the envious once-over. In restaurants there usually wasn't any problem, but at parties, where partners can get separated the moment they enter the door, Bill became angry with any man spotted standing closer than *two feet* from his date.

For game-players like Bill, *any* male response can be interpreted as a first, cunning step toward a planned seduction (except in those extremely rare instances where the player uses a woman—consciously or unconsciously—to attract men for *him*. In such an event there is a homosexual motive at work.). While no one likes to be caught in his own web, men like Bill seem to enjoy the way their women tempt other men, and often encourage it. Bill never got into any particular trouble beyond some embarrassing insult matches and the almost masochistic mental anguish he created by setting up such situations, but hospital emergency rooms and courts are filled with men who let the "game" get out of control.

More important than the danger involved, however, is the utilization of women as sex objects—*i.e.*, as things. There is little if any recognition that women are people with their own feelings and not mere enhancement objects for male egos.

The double standard has deeper ramifications. In a culture that sees some abilities—handling money, for example—as highly admirable, a woman who has such qualities and talent can pose a definite threat to a man's masculine identity. Bill showed off his girlfriends, then felt challenged when the efforts drew results. Similarly, many men are torn between boasting about their partners' competency and worrying that the *very same* competency menaces their masculinity. If she is assuming some of those supposedly "male" duties— and performing them *well*—in what other areas of the relationship has she taken the lead? In sex, perhaps? In making decisions, large and small? In *everything?* Fortunately there are men and women who are secure enough to enjoy cooperative rather than competitive relationships. The latter further feeds the destructive battle of the sexes which is unfortunately still prevalent in so many circles.

MORE ON ORGASMS

I can't let this chapter close without further mention of the orgasm. Women can—and do—sometimes enjoy sex *without* achieving orgasm. Some men simply don't care whether or not a woman climaxes, though the majority want to satisfy their partners. But then there are men who feel that the more orgasms a woman has, the better a lover he is, and lovemaking becomes a game to satisfy *his* machismo rather than the fulfillment of both partners' needs.

An abundance of orgasms all around is fine, but few men realize that their partners occasionally want merely to embrace or lie interlocked without even attempting passion leading to climax.

Chapter 7

Oedipal Feeling and Hostility

> I want a girl just like the girl that married
> dear old dad.
> —William Dillon, song

Men hate and fear that which they consider feminine in themselves. This does not endear women to them. How could it, when women are reminders of characteristics they harbor and resent? Yet, a man must make peace with the softer or so-called feminine aspects of himself in order to stop making war on women. Unfortunately, our culture continues to promote confusions about characteristics, proclivities and yearnings that are neither masculine nor feminine but only human.

After years of treating men, I've come to realize that a great many men really do not *like* women. They've been taught in innumerable and often subtle ways to fear women and to consider them as predatory and manipulative while at the same time seeing them as subservient, lacking strength of character, and generally falling into the category of intellectual lightweights. This negative paradox, coupled to undesired feminine feelings and dependency on women, must lead to hostility.

Men don't appreciate dependency—at least not when it's their *own*. Very few "cripples" (like the dependent medical student) are fond of the crutch they lean upon. This is why so many particularly or morbidly dependent men are unsatisfying lovers. While looking for good *sex partners*, they're also searching desperately for good *mothers*. Unresolved oedipal feelings lead to much sexual difficulty.

Regardless of their life-style, many men in our society are fighting their consciences all the time. "*Am I* doing this *right?*" they ask themselves at one moment. "*Should I* go ahead and *do* that?" *they* ponder at another. "*Could I* have dealt with this problem in a *better* way?" they wonder on a different occasion. Certainly these thoughts can be dismissed as minor, but taken as a whole, they add up to a very heavy weight.

Is it really any surprise that the very *last* thing most men want is to be evaluated by *someone else*—to be told what to do or what they did wrong? Too many men have double vision and can't make a distinction between their consciences and their partners'. As walking, talking extensions of the *male conscience,* women become authoritarian figures associated directly with a multiplicity of guilt feelings. If a man goes out and has a short affair with a woman and then feels he has to tell his wife in order to relieve his conscience, he has *made* his wife his conscience. As long as she remains his conscience—even if she has no idea that he has placed her in that role—he will resent her. If he has transferred his sense of conscience from his mother (and father) to himself and then to his wife, he will be both angry at his partner *and* extremely guilt-ridden, should he ever transgress.

WOMAN THE ENFORCER

Hostility toward women involves more than dependency, especially in neurotic men, and few people escape neurosis completely. Of course, the degree of neurosis and immaturity are most important in this connection. A wife represents both the good and the punitive mother. She *has,* after all, taken over for the man's real disciplining and demanding mother. It doesn't take much effort for him to switch his sense of moral prohibitions (what Freud termed superego) from parents to a wife.

Magically and quite thoroughly, the wife comes to embody symbolically all the externalized rules of our culture and civilization. She soon represents the demand for dealing maturely with responsibilities. There's the possibility that a man may even resolve these difficulties on a *conscious* level, but on a *subconscious* plane his need to remain a child, to be a playboy *without any responsibilities* other than to himself may persist.

Sexually, a wife can unintentionally place a burden on her partner, leaving him the impression that he has to *perform* rather than *participate*. A man in this psychological web not only rates himself, but is convinced that his mate is also tightening the vise. Having projected his outlook onto her, he finds that not only is *he* rating himself, but she seems to be doing so also. She's the "official" *scorekeeper*, and to make matters worse, she's also the punitive agent, armed and anxious to diminish him for not living up to the sexual standards he set for himself at the outset.

Consider this poor man—and he is quite ordinary—making love with a woman who represents judge, jury, jailer and enforcer for all the impossible sexual demands he makes upon himself. He's got to be what he envisions as a "real man"; sexually perfect, strong willed, and macho. With all this going on in him, hostility usually ensues.

On the one hand, the wife is *the* motivating cause for her husband's drive to establish and keep pace with the crazy standards he set for himself. On the other hand, she is his conscience. Because of her, there is nothing he can do to enhance his sense of masculinity without, at the same time, unleashing an avalanche of guilt. So concerned is he that his wife/conscience will get after him for any sexual wanderings, that he is unable to pursue any outside sexual adventures. Unfortunately, he often views an affair as the only means to feel renewed stimulation and to keep up with the sexual standards he wants to maintain in his relationship with his wife (and which he is absolutely convinced she is insistent upon). He's *supposed* to be faithful to her (no matter how popular the advocates of the "open marriage" concept may claim it's become, the percentage of marriages in which both partners condone extramarital affairs remains miniscule). *If* he's to be faithful to her, then *any* attempt to prove his manhood with another woman will produce guilt. And in the man's mind, who is the real guilt-producer? His *wife,* of course. Open talk regarding these issues can be helpful, but mostly this is only possible through a trained professional third party.

BOREDOM—WHAT CURE?

The demand for sexual performance in a marriage may continue well into the couple's sixties and beyond, creating a special dilemma. "We've been married for a long time," Margaret, a woman I know in her mid-fifties exclaimed quite proudly. "As the anniversaries came and went, we tuned in on each other's wavelengths more and more. I knew what Roy was thinking and wanting and feeling and he knew the same things about me. I guess you could say we fell deeper and deeper in love."

Roy, her husband, agreed. "We *do* love each other very much, but maybe we've grown to *know* each other too well. I suppose we've been together so long that recently I don't get excited by her anymore— physically, I mean. I love being with her, and holding her, but that old excitement isn't there."

Margaret and Roy were developing a very real problem—one that is unfortunately quite common. But what was there to do? Would extramarital relations be psychologically beneficial for a man like Roy? Would it bolster his confidence in his masculinity, spryness, and sexual ability? How destructive might it be to Margaret and her self-esteem? How would their relationship suffer as a result of these kinds of interventions? These are just a few of the problems inherent in this kind of situation. Other cultures have combined the stifling claustrophobia of the male myth with the unlimited freedom of polygamy or multiple relations. Ours promotes the myth, but outlaws even synthetic solutions. Under the rules most of us play by, men must be grand performers all their lives, but must be careful in seeking stimulating contrivances. This results in a considerable dilemma.

What happens to a man whose partner isn't understanding and willing to make all the extra efforts she can to allay these performance pressures? His desire for outside stimulation (even as an attempt to improve sex at home) generates self-hate if he is a conventional man. To make matters worse, he creates more self-hate by *not* pursuing these outside stimulants. To escape the pressure of this conflict he may attempt to shift the burden onto his wife. She may come to represent the external tyranny and the generator of his self-hate as he becomes increasingly hostile toward her.

Another possibility is also replete with complications. A wife who says, "Go ahead, do what you want, it's okay with me," sets herself up for equal criticism. If she *allows* her husband to have sexual relations with another woman, he may feel she no longer cares about him and that she is the destroyer of that all-important, pervasive romantic myth we reviewed in chapter 4. It's terribly difficult for a woman to win in either case *unless* her husband *grows up* emotionally and gives up performance in favor of real participation. That usually requires some form of professional analysis, and few men will take this alternative because they see it as just another indication of giving in to potential helplessness and, worst of all, *femininity*.

To avoid both guilt and analysis, many men may turn to prostitutes. With "play for pay" they're convinced they can receive all the necessary expert sexual stimulation without risking guilt feelings. A prostitute is a sex object who can generally be regarded as a special "non-woman" woman. It means very little to these men that the prostitutes aren't particularly any more expert in sex than a well-read, experienced wife may be. As we've seen, they certainly *aren't compassionate,* but the majority of men who use their services neither know this, nor, for that matter, care. Since "performance" is mainly used to support imaginary masculine attributes, prostitutes can be used in an attempt to bolster beliefs in continuing sexual prowess.

WHY CAN'T I DO THAT?

There is an interesting common resentment many men harbor but few admit. It's actually an unusual form of envy. Briefly put, they're annoyed at the female's power to attract and excite with sublimely simple acts: swaying breasts, for example, or just standing nude. Men don't usually have this "ability." In order to get sufficiently aroused to desire sexual intercourse, the great majority of women require *more stimulation* and even an *interest* in the man that goes beyond basic sexuality. Some, especially unconsciously passive men, envy the woman's ability to do her part by simply being there, while they in turn must be active and even assertive—in life, generally, as well as in sexual activity. The fact simply remains that men become excited with greater simplicity (often the sight of an attractive woman is sufficient) while women respond on a holistic and more complex level.

Chapter 8

Little Boys

Men are boys with longer legs.
—Anonymous

In most men there still lurks a little boy. There is much that is constructive and to be cherished about that little boy, but also much which is troublesome in terms of the adult world. It is this little boy who enjoys what some women consider juvenile activities: playing and watching baseball and football, telling dirty jokes, going bowling, hunting and fishing, joining clubs, reading adventure novels and watching science fiction movies. There is nothing wrong with any of these activities (which many women also enjoy), but sometimes they become the basis for a life-style.

For some men these entertainments are only small manifestations of the underlying little-boyhood that actually influences *everything* they do, whether it involves work and play or interaction with other men and women. Their immaturity affects *what* they do, *how* they do it, and often with *whom* they choose to do it. Few areas escape: neither earning a living, raising a family, playing gin rummy nor sharing love and sex.

Men find the idea that they are immature repugnant, since it implies vulnerability and dependency; it means not being in control at all times. Women aren't prepared to adapt to it, either. After all, what wife wants to concede that her husband approaches his business pursuits as a continuation of childhood gameplaying? Very dependent women are especially threatened by the idea of a "little-boy man." How can she depend on him?

Women's initial approach to the idea of pregnancy, birth and children makes them different from men in this regard. A woman makes an irrevocable commitment after the fifth month of pregnancy, in as much as she must go on to give birth. There is no turning back! This kind of basic, biological, irreversible decision has no parallel in men. This, plus the nine months' experience of pregnancy, as well as giving birth and providing the utterly dependent infant and young child with all that he or she needs, gives a woman a unique and maturing experience unknown to men. This is, after all, the foundation of life, on which rests the perpetuation of our species. I feel that this is the one area in which men and women are truly different. Despite a father's commitment and sense of responsibility to children and family, mothers are infinitely more closely identified with all aspects of the family matrix. This identification makes for a potential maturity and development largely unknown to men. This is rock-bottom, basic stuff, and perhaps the origin from which sprang the term "earth mother." All things being equal, I think most women harbor much less of the little girl in them than men do the little boy. Though there are exceptions, women, from my point of view, tend to be "earthier," more practical and less childish in their pursuits. In many women, all-important family business replaces the self-glorifying pride and egotistic pursuits common in many men. This aspect of continuing pressures from childhood dreams of glory— even more than a difference in physiology—may account for a shorter male lifespan.

A man provides a sperm, and this is of obvious practical importance and has for him symbolic significance too. Then as a father he can follow a career, repel invaders and win victories. He can engage in all the challenges that the world offers; he can become enormously successful; but he can't have a baby or be a mother. His commitment has not been of the basic nine-month biological kind, nor are his pursuits as important, however important they may seem in terms of society's peculiar hierarchy of values.

THE NEED FOR GROUPS

Since men frequently tow their adolescence with them into manhood, the souvenirs from younger days that they tuck into the back pockets of their memories include fears as well as hopes, brashness as well as sensitivity. Boys are easily frightened and put off by the possibility of female rejection. With the passing of years and the development of "maturity," many men find that they tend to back off from *anything* unfamiliar.

To relieve this anxiety, men often turn to continuing group association. They join a multitude of clubs, societies, organizations, fraternities and orders. In groups, they find a well-defined *hierarchy* that lets them know in *no uncertain terms* precisely where they stand in relation to those around them. Groups particularly allow men who have unresolved conflicts with their fathers, and who have not had intimate (nonsexual) relations with other men, a form of nonthreatening interaction and a way to measure themselves against others.

There's a certain power and reassurance not available to an individual *as* an individual, but there for the asking in many of the groups I've mentioned (this even includes community and religious-based men's clubs). Chain-link power—the power that suggests, "I'm someone to be reckoned with because my friends are there to support me on both sides and I can draw power from them"—and confidence overflow in groups that require ritualistic initiations, secret passwords and handshakes, regulation hats and full dress uniforms with insignia of rank emblazoned on shoulders and chests. At its most dangerous, that kind of power manifests itself in the form of underworld gangs, "families" and despotic political organizations, while at its most benign it is evident in adult fraternal organizations.

The "night out with the boys" is something else again. It can be a wonderfully healthy change of pace that allows a man breathing room, and on a *spontaneous* basis, is a good release. Ritualized, it's usually a yearning for escape and its participants more to be pitied than envied. A problem may be evidenced by a man who looks forward with eager anticipation to "going out with the boys" regardless of what his mood may be or whether or not "the boys" have any specific plans in mind. On an occasional basis, this escape route is understandable, but repeated regularly it may indicate a more serious inability to adjust to adult life.

Quite a few men actually prefer to be with other men. They just don't regard women as good company. "It's true, I *do* have more fun with the fellas," Ron, a rugged construction company project director told me. "I don't feel threatened by women [he *did*]; I can't say I always understand what they're all about [see chapter 4]; but I don't think I've got too much in common with them."

For men such as Ron, a sizable portion of social life and social aspirations revolve around—and involve—men. They spend their leisure time with men and rely on women purely for sexual and dependency needs. No wonder this attitude breeds resentment in wives and isolation between the sexes. This separation of the sexes begins in early life both at home and in the school and street. If society insists that certain interests and activities are feminine while others are masculine, a deep separation will be initiated. This feeling of difference and apartness continues to take on a life of its own in adolescent circles, where the fear of being called a "sissy" or a "tomboy" precludes communication between the sexes. This separation of the sexes makes for more than enmity. It also contributes to imaginary idealizations of sexy but pure fairy princesses and knights in shining armor. It likewise adds to confusion; aggression and sadism, for example, may be seen as masculine, while passivity and masochism are seen as feminine. In actuality these characteristics are simply human, albeit neurotic.

TEMPTATIONS

Childish emotions in would-be adults also manifest themselves in ways other than those discussed above. Male sexual frustration tolerance is seldom high. Now the feminist movement has equalized and reversed some roles so that many men feel intense pressure when their partners want sex and *they* don't.

The boyhood lure of "forbidden" sweets and childish curiosity makes it difficult for men to say no to other women who are new and appealing. It is often as simple a case as the lure of the strange and unknown, the need to devour experiences like gumdrops. So it is difficult, if not inconceivable, for some men to turn down the offer of a new body. After all, they might *never* get the chance again. And isn't it a *compliment* that they're being offered something for nothing? Surely *that's* a boost to synthetic self-esteem. It won't do much harm. . . . Who'll ever know?

Sometimes the man's partner can help to assure him that the options for continued originality, freshness, appeal and spontaneity in their relationship are alive and well. Of course the unfamiliar soon becomes familiar, but intensity and depth of experience are the stuff of prolonged and responsible relationships.

In some cases a husband looks to another woman because the quality of marital lovemaking has deteriorated or become ritualized. Communication is mandatory. If men can express their desires, needs, fantasies and fears to responsive wives, they may learn to deal with an exclusive commitment, even if tempted elsewhere.

Chapter 9

Anxiety and Guilt

There is another man within me that's
angry with me!
— Sir Thomas Browne,
Religio Medici II, *vii*

O coward conscience, how dost thou afflict
me!
— Shakespeare, *Richard III*

Guilt and anxiety are powerful enemies of sexual functioning and if pervasive enough can result in complete
absence of either sexual urge or ability to function.
There are any number of possibilities involved in the
origin of both anxiety and guilt, including unconscious
conflict, falls from ideal versions of one's self, hurt
pride and repressed anger. Most men have a relatively
poor tolerance for frustration and great sensitivity to
rejection or to any action which can possibly be interpreted as rejection. Many men also make claims
(often on an unconscious level) on women for un-
qualified total acceptance, regardless of how they
themselves behave. This, of course, makes for the
possibility of considerable anger any time temporary rejection (especially in the sexual area) or thwarting of
claims takes place. But men prideful of self-control or
fearful of disturbing the "nice guy" image or the
image of being perpetually rational and "adult" often
repress the anger they feel. Threatened emergence of
this anger to a conscious level often makes for considerable anxiety. If the anger is turned toward oneself
in a final attempt to repress it, guilty feelings and de-

pression will also ensue. Of course these feelings make sexual functioning very difficult, especially in relation to a lover who for the moment is unconsciously viewed as the perpetrator of difficulties in the first place. It is not easy to be a "good lover" and to combine tender open feelings with lusty sexual ones while in a state of rage, anxiety and depression, let alone to attempt to please and to pleasure the person with whom one is angry.

But what of the confusion, anxiety and guilt men suffer in terms of our society's so-called norms? This is a very important area for us to consider in terms of this book.

The discovery in us of urges, characteristics or desires which our culture may consider as perverse invariably produces guilt and anxiety. Yet, since we all start out as young children without cultural taboos of any kind, we continue to store a variety of residual uncensored feelings. I spoke of these earlier in referring to Freud's concept of "polymorphous perversus." Of course guilt and anxiety always affect our sex lives. Sex is, after all, a mirror reflecting how we relate to ourselves and to others generally, and it is a rather delicate and sensitive mirror.

Precisely *what* is "perverse" and "childish" again depends on the culture in question. Among certain groups, sex is *never* supposed to be used for any purpose other than procreation, while elsewhere it was —and still is—as common and relatively superficial an activity as shaking hands or saying hello. In Western culture, monogamy is the approved norm, while polygamy is actually *common* and *admired* in other parts of the world. If an individual could somehow base his life exclusively on either society's standards—or his own values—there'd be no problem. Since that's an impossibility, the mix of early feelings and thoughts and learned ideas often leads to guilt. In some of us it is negligible; in others, a hidden destructive force.

Of course much that causes anxiety in us goes on without awareness, having been repressed many years ago. Indeed, early influences of the most powerful kind

60

are sometimes buried too deeply to be available even through psychoanalysis. But these unconscious forces plus our continued efforts to repress them often make for behavior which would be inexplicable on a fully conscious, logical level. There are any number of boys and men, for example, who have been raised to believe that masturbation is a horrible activity (but who masturbate anyway) and who decry the practice in *others* as a means of purging themselves.

None of us is born with knowledge of our culture's mores or taboos; we have to learn them, and that learning process can be a trying experience. A man who says he is unable to recall childhood sex feelings and ventures may be suffering from guilt, strong inhibitions and a well-ingrained prudish attitude toward sexual feelings. *No one should have to look back on early sexual interest with guilt or recriminations!*

Still, so many men who look back would be astonished to find that what lingers in their memories as a terrible sin was nothing more than the same (or modified) normal sexual exploration undertaken by boys throughout the world.

One of the things women sometimes envy about men—the ability to urinate standing up—has served *most* young men as a perfect vehicle for comparison of each other's genitalia. What better way to see how developed another boy is than to stand next to him at a urinal and sneak a look over to his side? A *large* percentage of youngsters make comparisons and vie in other ways, including group masturbation (a common nighttime activity at summer camps). Testing who can urinate further is another means of comparison and an early test of sexuality and boyish macho. So, too, is a direct and unadorned comparison of penis size, which often proves to be the unfairest test of all for early and pre-teenagers (particularly those whose friends have already reached puberty).

If we single out masturbation, we've hit on the one activity that's almost *universal*. A man who feels guilty for having masturbated is only reflecting the inhibitions that were shackled onto him as he grew up.

Men also masturbate *after* they are married. Used at the right time, masturbation can serve as a very functional and practical aid to the happiness of *both* partners by reducing the physical and emotional tensions that a salesman away on a business trip or a husband whose wife is ill might not be able to relieve otherwise (except by sexual activity with another woman). A man burdened by guilt for having masturbated as a youth might find it *difficult* to stop the practice as a bachelor, but he'll have an *impossible* time dealing with the self-reprimands he'll give himself each time he does it *after* marriage. This kind of guilt and anxiety has a sexually inhibiting effect and may also lead to self-hate projected to his wife.

Masturbation is a natural practice that can be—and sometimes is—helpful if pursued even after marriage. There is nothing "wrong" with masturbation if a man feels like it or prefers it occasionally. Yet most men are certain that they must never prefer it to intercourse, and many feel debased and even demoralized each time they do it (there will be more on this in chapter 15).

GUILT

Sex lives can be good if *two* partners want and try to make them good and are cooperative with each other generally. However, standards are sometimes set too high, and this leads to disappointment, frustration, and misery.

Some very grandiose men and women take responsibility for their mates' moods. They blame themselves if a mood is bad or if there is a dampening of sexual interest for *whatever* reason; yet most such moods are due to an individual's own psychological histories and problems.

The sexual feelings, inhibitions and guilts we've

been discussing can cause adult reactions that range from minor irritation to severe anxiety and hostility. A man tortured subconsciously by his past is very liable to punish both himself and his partner in a futile attempt to eradicate his guilt. As Ebenezer Scrooge discovered, the mind is an easy place to haunt.

Chapter 10

The Penis: Symbol, Weapon, Delight

Love's mysteries in souls do grow,
But yet the body is his book.
—Donne, "The Ecstasy"

A sound mind in a sound body.
—Juvenal, *Satires* X

Though the intent of this book is to gain a better understanding of the psychological aspects of a man's sexuality, *mind* and *body* are intricately interrelated, and it's impossible to comprehend the psychological without also making sure that we have a reasonably uncluttered view of some of the physical aspects.

At the center of the male psychosexual life is the *penis:* mysterious, unique and fascinating; the object of potential pleasure and sometimes the cause of enormous unhappiness. Without question, it has *always* been a topic of the most intense fascination and there is evidence that the interest dates back to the very earliest days of mankind. Taken at random, a sample of the art and literature of any civilization is certain to provide a rich lode of documentary material. Paintings, sculpture, fiction and even historical writings abound with proof that the penis was highly regarded for both its practical *and* symbolic worth. A large penis was often a trait to be treasured and to be regarded with pride. As one of the differentiating characteristics possessed by men, it had meaning beyond the physical.

One of the best examples of its symbolic value dates back 3,200 years to the reign of King Menephta of Egypt. As reportedly detailed on a monument recording a great war victory, Menephta marched home with some trophies that were rather unique—the *penises* of six Libyan commanders and over six thousand Greek soldiers. The penises of another seven thousand or so enemy warriors were said also to have been removed.

Every male, at one period or another in his life, is concerned about the size of his penis. For many, that anxiety fades away following puberty, when the smaller dimensions associated with childhood expand into larger, acceptable adult proportions.

As we'll see, self-esteem underlies anxieties about size. There's a direct link between the way a man feels about himself (at home, on his job and in general) and how he views his penis. Overconcern can lead to a lifelong lack of confidence and may result in a vicious cycle of considerable gravity.

EARLY ROOTS

Nearly all anxieties involving penis size begin early in life and usually multiply for any number of reasons. First of all, before puberty, when a boy's penis *is* small, his parents may convey undue concern. This is especially true in cases where a father adheres to conventional macho dogma which, at least partially, rates a male on the basis of the size of his genitals, and in those cases where a father's own self-doubt has not been resolved. A boy induced to worry over his measurements during *pre-puberty* will frequently carry that image of inadequacy into *adulthood.* Secondly, as mentioned, a man's feeling that his penis is "too small" usually will coincide with his self-image at the time he makes the evaluation. Thus, if the center of his masculinity is symbolized by his penis, it will *seem* small whenever his personal esteem and sense of worth *is* small. Finally, many men have the mistaken notion that the penis ought to be large even when *not* erect. They read of the supposed dimensions of other men (often described in an erect state) and compare them with their own penis when flaccid. Furthermore, that comparison fails to take into account a number of crucial external factors and overall physical and psychological health.

Leonard, a twenty-five-year-old grade school teacher, had *never* slept with a woman. He even shied away from heavy two-way petting. "It's not because I haven't wanted to or haven't had the chance," he said. "It's just that my penis is *much too small* and I'm really embarrassed about what a girl might say." I wondered if perhaps Leonard was indeed "under-endowed," and asked him where he had gotten this impression.

"I don't know," he shrugged. "I guess in the high school locker room. After a few looks, I stopped comparing." After a few weeks of exploring problems of self-esteem, Leonard entered my office in a jubilant mood.

"You'll never guess what happened," he beamed. "Remember that girl, Rosemary, I've been going out with? Well, I finally got the courage to pursue our physical relationship. You know what? She actually said I'm *big*! And all that time I've been sweating about my 'problem'!"

A LOOK AT THE FACTS

Penis proportions are largely determined by genes and hormones. And penis size *isn't* standard in all parts of the world, nor, for that matter, from one segment of a population or specific group to another. It even varies among brothers.

Sometimes it is difficult to separate fact from fantasy. *Tall* men are thought to have larger penises than *short* men. *Black* men are believed to possess larger penises than men of other races. The mythology is staggering, and some studies run completely contrary to popular belief *and* scientific fact! One survey put the "average" range between five and ten and one-half inches, with blacks at the lower end of the scale, but those statistics are open to considerable criticism. Just as there are penises that are *larger than normal,* so too are there those *smaller* than found among the general population. Indeed, a condition of congenital hypoplasia, in which cell development inhibits the growth of a body organ, can in the *rarest of cases* cause the absence of the entire shaft portion of a man's penis so that the head of the organ is in direct contact with the pubic area.

For the vast majority of men, the flaccid penis (the penis is soft when used to empty the urinary bladder) measures from one to several inches long and about one inch in diameter. Dimensions vary according to air and body temperature (don't forget that nearly everything *contracts* in the cold) and mood. (A person suffering from anxiety will usually have a contracted penis; that's what often happens during an episode of impotence.) A penis tends, therefore, to hang its full length in *warm temperatures* and when a man is *relaxed.*

In practical terms, the length of an erect penis is *not* important to successful intercourse. Length may vary from man to man, but the significance rests only in *pride,* not *performance.* Furthermore (and this is so *very* important to many men like Leonard who silently criticize themselves when they see other men nude), small-looking, contracted penises often expand to a length *longer* than those that seem larger in the flaccid state. In addition, because of the perspective, a man's penis will appear smaller to him when he looks down at it than when he sees it in a mirror. Still, this is academic, since *most reach adequate and almost equal dimensions once aroused to full erection.*

At its longest, what doctors now consider the average erect penis measures six inches from base to tip, with a diameter of about one to one and a half inches. Angle, unless extreme, has no bearing on performance.

Some go up at forty-five degrees from the body, others slant to the right or left.

There are some societies, like ours, that place undue emphasis on penis size. The *length*—and ninety-nine percent of the people who discuss the subject *are* talking about length—is just about meaningless. Except for pressure on the cervix (which in rare cases can be exciting, but in many instances causes discomfort and pain), a woman can seldom determine how deeply a penis has penetrated her. Its diameter, however, may be meaningful in providing a sense of fullness. Some women are afraid, at least initially, that a penis may be too large, rather than too small.

Female orgasms are almost always triggered by the clitoris, which usually is best stimulated by the fingers or tongue. They can be started by such other focal points as the nipples, but this occurs on a rarer basis.

And, despite controversy, there is only *one* type of orgasm. It can, however, be experienced in *two* ways.

One, felt locally in the clitoris or the general vaginal area, is almost always a follow-up to clitoral manipulation. The penis doesn't have to be inserted at all and the sensation may be very *intense*. Another kind of reaction is *total* and is felt throughout a woman's entire body, so that it may be thought of as being global. It *may* follow direct clitoral stimulation, and sometimes may not be as intense as a local orgasm, although it has been described as *more satisfying*.

The global orgasm is often associated with a sense of vaginal fullness. The average vagina, remember, is a *relative* space, for the most part closed unless something is inserted in it.

A great many men seem to be confused about orgasms and actually feel remiss if they stimulate a clitoral response without vigorous use of the penis, but nevertheless the clitoris remains the seat of excitation.

The difference between a "normal" sized penis and one considered "large" becomes meaningless when viewed in terms of anatomy and physiology. The vagina is incredibly flexible and able to adjust to the diameter of *any* penis. The truth is, the average woman —if blindfolded—would be unable to tell the difference between penises of "average" and extra length! It's the psychological effect that counts, particularly if the woman has been taught to *believe* there is a difference, and if she has come to think of her own esteem—and that of her lover—in terms of a difference. Such a woman is prone to all sorts of wild theories about penis size. Once *objectivity* vanishes and a fantasy psychology takes over, the entire issue becomes *subjective*.

Lubrication also plays a major role in the sensation of fullness that so often determines a woman's impression of penis size. If the vagina is very lubricated, the penis will feel smaller (drying the penis once or twice during intercourse removes excess moisture and improves contact). The drier the vagina, the larger the penis is likely to feel.

There are some vaginas in which the penis *can* get lost, no matter how big it is, but this is rare and usually successfully treated by surgery. Position is also important; there are at least a few positions that make even the smallest penis feel adequate. Because other books have already provided detailed explanations, with drawings and photographs, I won't elaborate on mechanics here.

Interestingly, Freud based nearly all of his theory of the psychology of women on "penis envy"—the much-discussed notion that women have a desire to possess their own set of male genitals. Many believe that women don't actually want a penis as much as they want the respect and dignity it—and being a man —has always symbolized and provided.

DIFFERENT PERSPECTIVES

Women are not only *not* envious of the male for possessing a penis, but they are often remarkably (remarkable to men) uninterested in the penis in and of itself. They are uninterested primarily because they are tuned much more clearly than men into larger cultural values. They simply aren't as easily brainwashed by current trends (such as the host of graphic women's magazines) that emphasize penis size and male nudity. Generally speaking, *women are more complex than men,* less concrete and better able to view a man in general terms rather than merely according to his physical attributes. Consequently, men tend to be terribly concerned about the size of a woman's breasts or nipples (or whatever), while women make their judgments based on the *overall* man they see before them. A woman may get excited by the way a man talks or walks, by her feelings about his potential mastery, capabilities, articulateness, voice and so on— in other words, not by any *one* feature, but by a combination of some or all features and the kind of personality they may reflect.

From another point of view (and I'll only touch on this subject, since it involves the sexual psychology of women, but may serve to clarify an area of possible misunderstanding), women are very often influenced by the degree to which they feel they can *trust* their men. It has been demonstrated, for example, that her partner's penis size rarely has anything to do with a woman's problems in reaching orgasm. Men, in contrast, will complain, "If only my wife's breasts were *bigger,* I would be able to get it up more often." The woman, rather than being detoured from orgasm by a real or imagined lack of adequate penis size, fails to reach her peak (assuming that her clitoris has been adequately stimulated) because she has difficulty *trusting* her partner. Recent studies have revealed that women who have the greatest *problems* with orgasm are those whose fathers were viewed as not being *concerned parents.* The fathers who set limits ("Be home by eight o'clock") and show interest in their children as they grow from infancy to maturity tend to produce daughters who *are* orgasmic. The overly permissive or "detached" father may produce a daughter who is *not* orgasmic.

70

Once a woman has left the safety and "protection" of her parents in order to enter what can unconsciously be felt as a somewhat frightening and potentially destructive world, she has to transfer those particular feelings away from her father and apply them to her lover or husband. First she has to find a partner she *can* consider as her new, watchful, possessive father/lover/husband. Then she can believe that she *can* "let go" in orgasm and feel safe when she is in the relatively semiconscious and vulnerable state that orgasm may create. If, however, she thinks of her partner as basically weak, not "on guard" and even uncaring, she may not be able to let go.

Still, regardless of what we say to reassure men, many remain dissatisfied with their own size. They are frequently even jealous and fearful that their partners will find other men (with longer penises) more attractive and sexually adept. Young men fear that if a girl sleeps (or has slept) with other men she may never again be satisfied with either his sexual apparatus or sexual ability. Husbands dread the same thing about their wives. It's a basically childish attitude which ignores the fact that most makes a mockery of the concept that women look at men in the context of the *overall relationship* and not merely in terms of penis size and sexual ability. But unfortunately many men *insist* on believing that the length of their penises mirrors their masculinity and the range and intensity of emotional and sexual success they will share with the woman they love.

I noted in the section on dependency that wives very often become substitute mothers, unleashing all the complicated problems of dependency and punishment that permeate so many relationships. A man who is afraid of losing his partner to another man may really be frightened of losing his *mother* (as personified by his lover or wife). Any such loss—wife, lover, mother—can deal a *devastating* blow to his pride. Since we know the foundation of male pride is fragile at best, it's little wonder that these fears invariably instill anxiety, tension, and over-possessiveness in a

71

man. In the end, a couple's rapport has to suffer damage. It's a shattering realization to discover that you don't trust your partner, and perhaps an even greater blow to learn that *your partner doesn't trust you*.

MORE OF THE PHYSICAL

Once the penis is erect, it usually remains in that state until physical satisfaction is attained or the man loses interest in the stimulus. Distraction, or even too much stimulation, can cause the erection to disappear temporarily, although that generally is easily corrected by restimulation after a short delay. Very few (and I emphasize *very few*) men have the capacity for repeated erections immediately following ejaculation. Interest and erectile ability do increase as time increases from the last ejaculation, but this period, too, is highly individual and can vary from hours to days, depending on mood, fatigue, the setting, stimulation and sexual possibilities.

Far too many women (as well as men) don't know about this variation in recuperative powers. Merely because a man reaches orgasm, ejaculates and is able to sustain an erection fifteen minutes later doesn't necessarily mean he'll be able to do the same thing the next time. It may take him *twice as long* or even a *few days*. The same is true in reverse. I've known numerous single, sexually experienced men who were unable to achieve an erection during their first attempt at lovemaking with a particular woman and found that they were never given a second chance to try. A partner who is understanding, who realizes that the man is pressured by his whole upbringing to "prove" himself, and who is aware that mood, fatigue, or setting may be having a negative effect *at that instant,* can sometimes rescue the situation. She must reassure her lover that there is no problem, that he should relax, and that they'll make love the *next* time. Most wives *know* their husbands' good and bad moods (and when he is tired or upset) but many *aren't able to read the telltale signs* even after years and years of marriage. The inability to achieve and sustain erection usually reflects a problem on the part of the man of psychological origin but soon becomes a mutual problem. This is why most sex therapists agree that treatment of both partners as a marriage unit is most effective.

ERECTIONS

While it is safe to generalize that young men are usually capable of higher erectile frequency than more mature men, this *isn't always true.* I have heard of men who had a second orgasm with the same erection, but I'm sure this is exceedingly rare in men of any age. I noted earlier that recovery time depends on a number of external and internal factors as well as on age. Even if they could, most men, having lost the sense of novelty of earlier sexual adventures, find it strenuous and even *unpleasant* to attempt rapid multiple erections and ejaculations. Yet I've seen a number of men in consultation who felt that anything *less* than several orgasm-ejaculations in a night was a sign of waning desire and creeping senility. Regrettably, many women agree just because they don't know any better. To make matters worse, they start to look and act critically, even contemptuously, at a partner who is unable to maintain the height of ardor and sexual prowess he achieved in the first years of their relationship. *Once upon a time,* the man *may* have been at that level. He may still be trying to stay there rarely because his partner is not understanding and, more likely, because he has a *false* idea of what constitutes manhood. Often these ideas come directly from novels and movies that portray *fictional* "studs" in action.

Normally erections disappear moments after ejaculation, although some men are able to maintain a semierect penis for a short while. There are some few women, however, who either don't understand or don't care about physiology and insist that the man keep his stiff penis in the vagina *all night* before or without ejaculation. For whatever reason, they don't accept the fact that it is terribly difficult for a man to sleep in that state of excitement. When their partners refuse, the women act angry or hurt. They are even more demanding when they request that the man keep his penis in the vagina *after* he has ejaculated. That, to put it bluntly, is usually impossible.

A woman may also be confused or misled when she notices that her partner is getting an erection while he sleeps. Those erections are cyclical and seem to be related to physiological need and the dream process.

Erections pose another dilemma that is easy to understand but difficult to resolve. On the one hand, if a woman is unappealing the man may have greater staying power because the stimulus is not as exciting as it might be. If, on the other hand, the partner is *very appealing,* the man may become more excited. Thus, the unfortunate man who is with a partner who excites him (precisely the type of woman he wants to enjoy a sexual experience with for an extended period of time), will be triggered to orgasm and ejaculation far more rapidly than the man who is bored by his unattractive partner and who strongly desires to complete the encounter as quickly as possible.

A full bladder, by the way, will sometimes cause an erection. This is especially noticeable in the morning if the man has not urinated during the night.

ORGASMS AND EJACULATION

For centuries, poets and writers have called on every imaginable adjective and turn of phrase to describe orgasm. Simply put, it's a *total* experience, unlike ejaculation, which is a purely physical release—a spurting-out of seminal fluid. Orgasm occurs in the generalized musculature and leads to an allover response (unlike ejaculation's local sensation) that prompts muscular contractions, heightens blood pressure, and speeds up the pulse. Perhaps even more important is the intense emotional release that accompanies orgasm but is absent in simple ejaculation.

There are differences between the male and female sexual responses. Women often take longer to *get* aroused and then *stay* aroused longer, can sometimes experience multiple or repeated orgasms, and lose their sexual urges and sensations over a greater period of time than do men. For the male, sex is a *more concentrated* event, building to the one ultimate and powerful climax. Once ejaculation has taken place, tension and energy are exhausted, and a calm sets in. With few exceptions, most men who experience orgasms and then seek to go to sleep are *not* demeaning their partners. Their response is physiologically preordained.

Men just about always ejaculate during orgasm. Recent study indicates that some men experience orgasm (a generally heightened physiological and emotional response) without ejaculation too, but this is relatively rare. It is true that some men do not achieve ejaculation *or* orgasm, even after prolonged intercourse, but in cases like those, psychological factors are usually to blame.

It's another question entirely when we try to compare the varying degrees of intensity at which men experience orgasm. Reactions can range from a narrowly localized, pleasurable sensation to an encounter draining enough to border on unconsciousness. The variation in intensity could be greater for many men if they released inner emotions by moaning, sighing, yelling, laughing or even screaming with pleasure, if that's what the orgasm made them feel like doing. Here again, *women* generally feel freer to let loose. They're certainly not afraid of seeming feminine and don't seem to worry about ruining their image by demonstrating "lack of control" with a partner they trust. I've also known women whose husbands or lovers were *so* Victorian in their thinking that the women refrained from showing pleasure for fear of what their men might think, thus destroying spontaneous and natural reactions.

The height of sensation in the penis usually occurs in the fraction of a second preceding ejaculation, with lesser sensations occurring in the three to eight or so contractions that follow as semen is ejected. There are *many men* who actually regard *each* contraction as a separate *orgasm* and then boast to friends that they "came five times," when in reality the five ejaculations were the result of *one orgasm* and *one* ejaculation.

Because the entire ejaculatory process is under the control of the spinal reflex, it's really somewhat like knee-jerking—it can't be controlled once it's touched off. On the average (and this figure varies according to the interval between orgasms and other factors) the total seminal fluid amounts to about one quarter of a teaspoon. It is normally at body temperature, viscous, relatively tasteless (slightly salty, possibly bitter), usually colorless, and filled with a great number of sperm cells. It is perfectly safe to swallow and contains few calories. Swallowed, it doesn't cause weight gain, illness or pregnancy.

While the sperm count (*i.e.*, the number of sperm in a given amount of ejaculatory liquid as seen under a microscope) will have *no* effect on a man's ability to achieve an erection and reach orgasm with ejaculation, it *may* hamper his efforts to successfully fertilize an egg. A couple who are trying to conceive a child, and who find after a reasonable period of time that they're having no success, should be examined to see whether they've had bad luck or a medical problem.

No matter how much they want children, many men *refuse* to have such an examination. It is that terrible, unfounded terror that an adverse report will reflect on their masculinity. In large part these men confuse virility, sterility, potency, and sexual ability.* They only hurt themselves, and their wives, when they fail to

* Potency refers to ability to maintain an erection. Virility and sterility are terms used to indicate ability to fertilize an egg and impregnate a woman. Ability obviously refers to lovemaking, including sexual intercourse.

realize that sperm count plays no *physical role* in either improving or downgrading male sexual ability. The psychological effect, on the other hand, can be serious and paralyzing.

Nature's *primary* interest in sexual functioning has always been to *perpetuate the species*. If pleasure has been present, it has probably been put there as an added inducement and to enhance the sexual urge. Eons ago, nature couldn't foresee the advent of controlled propagation and the shift toward sex for *pleasure* instead of for practical reasons. For that reason, nature made pregnancy as likely as possible by placing an enormous number of sperm in each ejaculation and by making ejaculation involuntary once underway.

The entire ejaculatory process is liable to variations for all the reasons already cited. Some men who are prone to ejaculate quickly use thick condoms or numbing cream to lessen sensations in the penis and improve control. Others enjoy being stimulated to one degree *short* of orgasm before stopping and starting all over again. Unfortunately, as many doctors have found, that sort of "teasing" can lead to prostatic difficulties, a result that isn't worth *any* pleasure, no matter how intense. A great many men plagued by quick ejaculation *masturbate* a few hours before intercourse to alleviate pressure in the seminal ducts. There's danger here, too, of course. Any one of the affecting factors (most prominently fatigue) can occur *before* intercourse takes place. If that happens, it may become *impossible* for the man who has "weakened" the seminal and nerve pressure by masturbating to achieve an erection for actual coitus.

By the way, it's interesting to note that the fluid that seeps out of the penis before ejaculation *doesn't* (as some men and women believe) detract from the ejaculation. It serves merely as a cleanser of the urethral track to allow the speeding sperm a safe trip up and out.

Misinformation, especially in pornographic books, insists that *women's orgasms are accompanied by ejaculation*. This is not true! Women don't *need* them (the egg needs no fluid to carry it to the site of fertilization), and female anatomy does not provide for ejaculation. Despite that, sexy and pornographic novels describe women of marvelous responsivity who literally inundate their partners and themselves in seas of orgasmic discharges. The fluid a women does exude comes only from her *lubricating* glands, and the amount is hardly enough to cause the flood reported in such vivid detail in erotic literature.

CIRCUMCISION

Circumcision (properly done, of course) can only *help* a man, not *harm* him. And it's beneficial from both a *medical* and *sexual* standpoint. In fact, it's been considered so important throughout the ages that it's believed to be the *oldest known surgical operation*. Archaeologists have discovered circumcised Egyptian mummies, wrapped and hidden in tombs for more than three thousand years.

According to the Bible (1 Sam. 18:25), David, in love with King Saul's daughter Michal, became one of the world's best known amateur practitioners of circumcision when his future father-in-law requested a special dowry: *the foreskins of one hundred Philistines.*

Today, even discounting its enormous religious and mystical significance, circumcision *remains* the most frequent form of surgery. But why?

First, it eliminates the strong possibility of serious infections, irritations and even gangrene (which may result in loss of part or all of the organ). The latter may occur as the result of the foreskin's swelling around the shaft, cutting off necessary blood circulation. Second, as statistics prove, it lessens the woman's chance of contracting cervical cancer, a malady that some gynecologists feel may be caused by irritating dirt lodged under the foreskin. Recent researchers feel that some uncircumcised men transmit a virus that plays a role in cervical cancer.

Male infants are circumcised as a matter of course shortly after birth; adults can have the procedure performed on them in a relatively simple surgical procedure. Some men experience passing impotence after the operation, but the number of those affected in such a negative psychological way is minimal. In almost all cases, the psychological effect is actually positive (since fears of medical calamities resulting from non-circumcision are alleviated), and the physical healing process is quick and complete. Sexually, most people able to make a comparison feel that there is no difference in the intensity of the sensations of circumcised and uncircumcised penises. On a preventive basis, men who have undergone the simple procedure are less likely to develop infections that would physically hamper their sexual performance. On a psychological level, a woman who realizes that she stands less of a chance of developing cervical cancer from a circumcised man may be less tense and thereby able to feel freer in sexual intercourse.

CASTRATION

Some classical Freudian psychoanalysts feel that fear of castration and dreams of castration ("castration anxiety") are more concrete than symbolic; that men actually do fear injury or loss of genitals. Many psychoanalysts feel otherwise. I have found that castration anxiety, particularly in dreams, is related to hurt pride resulting from business reversals, failure in examinations, etc., so that castration anxiety is of high *symbolic* consequences, and usually related to an attack on self-esteem.

In times past, however, castration was not merely symbolic. It was, of course, a popular form of torture, and was also used much like gelding to "take the fight out" of potential slaves. Eunuchs who had been castrated served in harems and young boys of the seventeenth century were turned into permanently high-pitched choir and opera singers by the gruesome operation. There were even members of a religious sect in Russia who considered emasculation the *key to heaven*.

Chapter 11

Homosexuality—
Lifestyle/Nightmare

It may be that we can act as we choose,
but can we choose?
Is not our choice determined for us?
    —J. A. Froude, *Spinoza*

Homosexuality has come partway out of the closet. In recent years, its tortured ascent has elevated it to a shadowy level where a mix of subtle and candid education now permits most adults to acknowledge its existence. And yet, sad to say, most of us remain centuries away from the kind of enlightenment that would make the issue a non-issue. Because no amount of arguing will alter the power of tradition and the Bible, the fear of homosexuality remains ingrained in the heterosexual unconscious.

Homosexuality, of course, has been around a long time. With barely an exception in our culture, it has been considered the sin of sins, perversion, antisocial rebellion and an illness. It has been deemed the evil corrupter of youth and morals and the death knell for entire civilizations.

HOMOSEXUALITY: ITS DEVELOPMENT

Homosexuality is a special adaptation and from my point of view is, like other symptoms, a function of anxiety. Many homosexual men explain that they better after a sexual contact because it makes them feel more *adequate* as human beings, as well as less anxious. Unfortunately, considerable self-hate often follows too. Homosexuality is *more* than merely the attraction of men for other men. It's really an attraction to a whole way of life—to being with men and a society that understands and accepts the homosexual psychology. *Our* society, for all of its supposed liberalism and modernity, still pays little more than lip service to the concept that everyone can choose his own life-style as long as it doesn't interfere with anyone else's.

Unfortunately just what causes homosexuality continues to be one of medicine's most intensely argued subjects. Most experts believe, as I do, that *upbringing* dictates the sexual direction a youngster will take. The strong mother, weak father argument is well known, but even *that* combination is open to debate. Many men grow up heterosexual in spite of these odds, and there are numerous instances where the older and younger brothers of homosexual boys have never been anything but heterosexual. In such families, the individual child's direct relationship with his mother—the degree of her influence and hold on him—is probably the deciding factor as to which road he will choose. Homosexuality can also be fostered by intense *self-rejection* in a boy who has not gained sufficient confidence in himself, by a *contempt for masculinity* shown by either or both parents (and by parents who wanted a girl but got a boy instead), or by a generally inadequate sexual environment.

Singling out self-rejection, we've got to be mindful that homosexuality *doesn't just happen.* It takes as much development as heterosexuality and doesn't occur, as many people wrongly believe, because a boy is seduced by an older man and led down the "sordid path to degradation and perversion." A man who rejects his sexual identity (through homosexuality, transvestism, transsexuality, asexuality) rejects a major part of himself. As such, from my point of view, homosexuality must be described as a form of self-hate.

HOMOSEXUALITY TO HETEROSEXUALITY

There are those people and groups who would have the rest of us believe that all homosexuals are really heterosexuals trying their best to escape a terrible burden. This is, of course, patent nonsense. Male homosexuals tend to have a tremendous resistance to any idea of giving up homosexuality. In fact many heterosexual males falsely believe that homosexuals are a *neuter gender* and have virtually no existence *as sexual creatures*. Homosexuals, at the same time, *don't* believe that surrender of their sexual preference will lead to heterosexuality. They usually (often unconsciously) see *asexuality*, not heterosexuality, as the unavoidable alternative. The idea that asexuality may result is terribly frightening and anxiety-provoking because it also suggests the removal of *any* possibility of great emotional closeness to other human beings. For the homosexual, as for the heterosexual, asexuality is somewhat akin to nonexistence and is a terrifying thought. Homosexuality is actually an *advanced* stage of sexuality, and the homosexual man has well-defined sexual interests, urges and proclivities at least as complicated as his heterosexual counterpart. Interestingly, many asexual men often have to pass through a period of homosexuality before they get to a heterosexual stage.

There are *some* homosexual men who do give up their homosexuality, but this is relatively rare—on a lasting basis—without long and trying analysis and therapy. Most homosexual men who voluntarily undergo psychological treatment do so *not* because they want to become heterosexual, but because they are depressed, anxious or burdened with any one of the many different problems that affect every segment of the general population. In therapy many of these men emphasize that they want to get rid of the particular problem but don't want their homosexuality changed or erased. Occasionally, when psychotherapy continues for an extended period, patients feel freer and more willing to probe the sexual area. In a handful of those instances, homosexuality is worked on and may, eventually, be surrendered in favor of heterosexuality.

There are any number of homosexual men who make an heroic effort toward a heterosexual adjustment in an attempt to comply with standards of family and society. Many marry and try to conform to heterosexual values. For some, the adjustment endures if a girlfriend or wife is understanding and there aren't any significant self-esteem setbacks at home or at work.

From time to time, however, certain tensions and anxieties may become unbearable. A man may be unable to resist an internal, unconscious pressure to please himself and relieve his sexual tension in what he feels is his "real" direction. The only way many homosexual men who are attempting to reject their homosexuality and to lead a heterosexual life feel they can successfully cope is to go "cruising," to seek out and consummate a male-male sexual encounter. In providing himself with a momentary surge of genuine (or synthetic) self-esteem, some Freudians would say such an individual is searching for a penis because he feels he lacks an adequate one of his own. I think a broader and more accurate interpretation might be that he doesn't see any value in the esteem of women, but *does* see it in men. From a purely symbolic viewpoint, therefore, a strong male is very important to him. If he can seduce a male symbol, then for a moment, at least, he is the recipient of power and has temporarily enhanced his own self-esteem. Having done this, he can once again return to his heterosexual life.

In clinical experience, most therapists find that homosexuals who have had *some heterosexual* encounters are more capable of renouncing their homosexuality than men who have never shared sex with a woman. The heterosexual experience, even if buried deep in the memory, is an indication of *some* heterosexuality and usually also indicates (unless he was *forced* into the encounter) less fear of it.

Some men—heterosexual all the way—do occasionally attempt to manipulate women in a peculiar way. Keep an ear open in any of the singles bars that line New York's East Side and eventually you may hear at least one "homosexual" young man telling his troubles in the "queer" life to a sympathetic-looking, probably beautiful and sexy, decidedly heterosexual young lady. It's a ploy that certain heterosexuals rely on in the hope that their new-found female companion will first convince them verbally, then physically, that heterosexuality really is the *better* way. Who knows how many "homosexuals" have been "reformed'" by dedicated female missionaries on the Heterosexual Crusade?

INNER FEELINGS

Real homosexual men don't go seeking that kind of solace over a few drinks at a crowded singles bar. Not at *most* singles bars, anyway. The same isn't true at establishments that cater strictly to homosexuals. But then, homosexuals aren't very well understood by people who don't share that life-style. Many therapists feel that homosexual men have more anger than heterosexual men, a great deal of which is repressed. Some analysts believe that this is due mainly to feeling deprived by an uncaring father and exploited by an overpowering, stifling mother. A great number of homosexual men who are hostile to women—and that includes many—sometimes reveal it in the fashion and hairstyles they create, neither of which allow women to look like women (or men) when everything is said and done.

Still, I've seen quite a few homosexual men who had better person-to-person relationships with *women* than with *homosexual friends,* let alone heterosexual men. Some even surpassed heterosexual men in establishing relationships with women. It's intriguing to postulate just why these surprising friendships do form, and a discussion with half a dozen men and women of both sexual persuasions might easily turn up quite a few very solid, very different reasons. It may be that homosexual relationships are often so turbulent and highly competitive, so filled with claims, envies and jealousies, that the men look elsewhere for friendships. If this is the case, then relationships probably don't develop with heterosexual men who tend to feel extremely threatened by homosexuality and don't want to risk *any* contact, whether platonic or otherwise.

Women, however, don't feel threatened (either sexually or socially) by homosexual men and can be more open to any overtures in the direction of friendship. There's an interesting twist here, too. It seems, at first, incongruous that anyone carrying around a storehouse of hostility toward women would want to be friends with any members of that sex, yet there are a percentage of homosexual men who seem to maintain a relatively high degree of respect for women and not nearly the amount of male chauvinism that their heterosexual colleagues like to flout. This probably stems in large part from residual strong feelings of closeness and respect felt for their mothers, whom at the same time they hate (often unconsciously).

Talent and Homosexuality

As noted, homosexual men usually place their homosexuality at the *very center* of their life-style. It affects their occupations as well as their relationships with other people. Why this happens no doubt has more to do with our society's negative view than with anything else. Because of that view, prejudices abound, among them the idea that certain artistic, non-athletic activities are antimasculine, if not outrightly homosexual.

There's a belief shared by many adults that homosexual men, as a group, are *more talented* than heterosexual men. A quick look at the field of interior decorating or hairstyling shows that these areas do seem to be dominated by male homosexuals. It could be argued that homosexuals dominate these fields because they *are* more artistic. But it's more likely this domination exists simply because homosexuals aren't afraid of doing certain work other men avoid because they associate it with homosexuality. Homosexuals appear more talented because they are *less repressed* in so-called feminine areas. Obviously, once they make the "admission" that they're homosexual, they no longer have to maintain a false front of macho virility. They can dispense with the myth of masculinity and get on to doing what they *want* to do, not what society would have them do. Free of the shackles worn by heterosexual men, they can be decorators, hairstylists and ballet dancers. Not caught in the web of cultural tangles, they can show emotions, play with flowers, sew, cook and do all the things most heterosexual men, terrified at the thought of being labeled "homosexual," would do only under duress.

Heterosexual men might have the same inclinations and might be just as successful and creative with these interests and occupations, but because of their fear of homosexuality they repress those leanings and kill off their creative possibilities, leaving the impression that they are, indeed, less talented.

APPEARANCE AND HOMOSEXUALITY

One of our culture's more popular, though rarely discussed pastimes, is a game I'll call, for want of a better name, "homosexual watching." It's a bit like girl watching, except that in that game there rarely is trouble deciding whether a *female is a female*. Girl watching is more or less a blend of visual observation leading to fantasy appreciation and pleasure. Homosexual watching is more complex since it first calls upon the players to: (1) decide whether or not a man *is* homosexual; (2) judge the degree to which he is; (3) study him as he goes about doing whatever he's doing, including merely walking down the street;

and then (4) comment derogatorily to a companion. Most people would deny they ever involve themselves in this particular amusement because, laid out before them, it appears to be just what it is: cruel, nosy and tactless. Still, most people do play, to one degree or another, even if they only half-consciously follow through the first two or three steps of the game.

Appearances, however, can be quite deceiving. Effeminate-looking men are not necessarily homosexuals, nor are rugged, deep-voiced truck drivers necessarily all heterosexuals. Foppish men may not have the slightest inclination toward others of their own sex, but may have been raised with many sisters, who made it easy for them to pick up some of the outwardly feminine mannerisms that later provide a basis for false impressions.

There are, at the same time, men who are very effeminate in the way they talk and act who actually *would* like to be women. *Transvestites* often fit into that category, although an individual's desire to wear women's clothes still doesn't mean he definitely is a homosexual. A *transsexual* is a man who undergoes surgery in order to become a woman to the greatest extent possible, but the transvestite, who is sexually a male, is usually content to dress up occasionally like a lady. In the second case, experts would classify the desire as a *fetish* and, while many men with fetishes are basically homosexual (sexual excitement aroused by women's shoes), *all men are fetishists to some extent*. But some fetishes are more socially acceptable than others. For example, the man who likes to see his wife in lingerie is a fetishist, but he is less condemned by society than the man who enjoys kissing his wife's shoes or seeing her dressed up in an outlandish costume of one sort or another.

Long hair on young men is certainly not a sign of homosexuality either, yet not too long ago countless men and women made value judgments about men they saw for the first time purely on the basis of hair length. Some otherwise mature adults who may think they believe otherwise, still *feel* that long hair is not

hininity. Let me explain. With only rare excep-
it's the mother who takes care of the children
nfancy to adulthood, and no matter what efforts
de to counter the effect, little boys and little
an't help but identify with mother and the
e role.

the young girl, the progression is smooth and
While she may have problems separating her-
as an individual different from her mother,
sn't have to make a break in terms of sexual
ation. The young boy, on the other hand, is
th a greater task. Not only does he have to
himself that he is an individual and therefore
e person from his mother, he has to shift his
entity. Much research has been done in this
experts now believe that the boy must make
and identify with his father, another male or
y in general by his *second* birthday. If the
hasn't been made by that age, associations
ifications become harder to sort out and run
e risk of entrenching themselves even deeper
rs go by.

angeover doesn't always take place. It is
cult in a household with a domineering
d a weak and virtually absent father—the
non combination that seems to be the best
for the development of a homosexual pre-
, as I've mentioned before, the father can't
and the mother is equated with strength,
oy may then equate strength with feminin-

a youngster can make the necessary sep-
mother—and our culture contributes to
n—is by creating the feeling that he is
omen. By differentiating himself even more
he can combat the dual fear of non-differ-
the potential misidentification his mother's
ght have imposed on him. As long as he
s air of superiority—and it's a *lifelong*
most cases—he need never worry about
to childhood vulnerability. To create this

quite masculine and are responding to the influence
of a symbol well entrenched in the unconscious. Many
men wear their hair long these days not because they
particularly like it themselves, but because they've
discovered that it stimulates *women*.

Every generation has its own antiestablishment, antiauthority way of dressing, grooming and acting. Very
frequently, if enough people try to be *nonconforming,*
the very means they take to achieve that goal becomes
the *conforming* thing to do. Neither hair length, nor
any other characteristic, indicates sexual preference.
Homosexuals themselves are not attracted to any
one type of man. Some like partners with long hair,
others with short; some like men with smooth skin,
others prefer bodies covered with hair. Some go for
masculine-acting men, others are drawn to very effeminate partners. Variation is the same as when measured
against the range of attraction of heterosexual men to
women with blue or brown eyes, blond or brunette
hair, big breasts, long legs and so on.

Another false indicator sometimes used to gauge the
presence of homosexuality is a man's inability to be
forceful; to stand up to his employer or to friends.
Here again, this has absolutely nothing to do with
homosexuality, but usually only stems from a poor
sense of self-esteem. If a man has doubts about himself, he will have doubts about his ideas and he'll back
down whenever he faces a more assured adversary.
Many heterosexual men are incredibly *compliant* people, while many homosexual men are assertive, and
aggressive.

FEAR OF HOMOSEXUALITY

Put into proper perspective, homosexuality is not
quite the problem it might seem to be—at least not
to homosexuals themselves. The *fear* of homosexuality
is something else again, and poses a considerable problem for a great number of heterosexual men. Why else

do comedians joke about it, playwrights invent laugh-provoking adventures around it, and young boys and men tease about it with an overdose of flipness and a heavy helping of cruelty? They do it because underneath the devil-may-care abandon, the sly and sometimes coarse humor, the lisps, exaggerated limp wrists and overly swaying hips, "straights" hide very real fears. Some get over it at a relatively early age, but for a great many men in this country, homosexuality poses a threat usually present under only minimal repression. The *fear* far outweighs *reality* but continues as an extremely prevalent concern in our male population. Many men will do anything they can to avoid giving anyone the impression that they are latent homosexuals.

Not all societies regard homosexuality with the same terror, of course. What to us may seem obscene or deviant has for centuries been viewed by some cultures in the Near East as acceptable and unworthy of mention or second thought. At the same time, what might seem appealing and quite normal to us—miniskirts, for instance—is considered perverse and immoral elsewhere.

But in our society men often compensate in terms of sexual bravado and so-called masculine pursuits in order to avoid even the slightest doubt from themselves and others that they are in any way tainted. It must be remembered that to many heterosexual men homosexuals are not male, not female, but a neuter gender devoid of any sexuality and without proper human identity at all.

There's an interesting sidelight to this point which I'd like to illustrate for a moment. You'd expect that a man, discovering his wife or girlfriend in a *lesbian* affair, would be angry and threatened by the presence of a third person in what should culturally be a strictly one-to-one, male-female relationship. Some men may react that way, but many don't equate female homosexuality with its male counterpart. They often do not take female sexuality seriously. Some men see it as nothing more than a prank of passing interest to

the women involved and not som
ing over. Why? I believe that it i
think female sexuality is of itse
their lesbianism is also unimport;
man finds it much more difficult
covery that his partner is enga
relationship, because that const
unlike the "harmless" if annoyi
lesbianism. In the latter his m
hurt.

Heterosexual men, as we'll s
fears of homosexuality in m;
situations. A business revers
self-esteem may evoke homo
homosexual fantasies and ho;
ever harmless and routine, c
the opportune moment to co;
who suffer from impotence, f
it with homosexuality, eve
nothing at all to do wit
have proven, homosexual n
ally aggressive and potent a;
parts. The objects of sexu
and devotion differ, but
failure" interest is as pow

The fear of homosexua
helplessness and is equate
as antimasculine. Calling
self-derisive way (*e.g.*, ir
a form of self-hate prom
men that this is, in effe
be. Of course the conf;
ceptions accumulated s

MEN AND C

Growing up, as w
It is more difficult fo
of masculinity than

of fer
tions,
from i
are m
girls c
femini
For
direct.
self ou
she do
identific
faced w
convince
a separa
sexual ic
area, anc
the break
masculini
transition
and identi
the genuii
as the yea
The ch
more diffi
mother an
most comn
foundation
dilection. I
be relied o
the young b
ity.
One way
aration from
this distortic
superior to w
than needed,
entiation and
early care m
maintains thi
protection in
slipping back

fictional self-image, he accepts or rejects any real differences that exist to his advantage and actually makes up new ones that don't exist on a *biological* level, but which he's pressured into believing on a *cultural* level. Physical strength, therefore, isn't enough in and of itself. Greater intelligence, superior judgment, and other less tangible but more important factors are added to the fictional mix. *Male chauvinism* and the *myth of masculinity* are the next steps in this kind of progression. Feelings and sensitivity aren't permitted to flourish within the confines of the myth, nor is weakness or fallibility, either on an emotional or logical plane.

FEAR OF DISCOVERY

It takes very little impetus for many heterosexual men to worry seriously about masculinity or the sort of manly impression they make on *other* people. But homosexual men and women continue to fear discovery, too. A recent study found that approximately *half* of all admittedly homosexual men and women are at one time or another afraid of being "discovered" by acquaintances. Women become less and less concerned with discovery as they enter middle age (the survey estimated that only ten percent remain fearful), while a substantial number of males (twenty-five percent) continue to worry.

DISPLAYING AFFECTION

As I've mentioned, fear—*real fear,* whether conscious or unconscious—very often dictates the things men do. As indicated earlier, the man who is afraid of doing anything that might be interpreted as homosexual makes every effort to behave in the most masculine manner. Perhaps one of the most obvious examples of this phenomenon appears in the command-suggestion little boys receive from their fathers: "You're a big boy now; you're a *man,* and *men* don't kiss other men; they shake hands! Show Uncle John what a *big man* you are and go over and give him a nice strong handshake!" By age seven or eight, this thinking is so ingrained in the boy that showing affection for other men (including his father) is extremely difficult. *Any* male-oriented affection has to be kept hidden. I know quite a few men who were deeply troubled by this and became *extremely* unhappy whenever they encountered a situation that posed the dilemma.

Stephen and Robert, who came from different parts of the country, shared *opposite yet identical* problems.

Stephen, a lawyer, had been raised in a Midwestern town by quiet parents who looked upon hard work and a rewarding good pat on the back as the ideal operative sequence of a man's life. In his family, women could kiss men, of course, and women could kiss other women (platonically on the cheek), but *no one dared even consider the possibility* that men could quite naturally greet each other with a hug or kiss on the cheek. When Stephen met Heidi, there was a conflict. Born in Switzerland and brought to the United States by her parents when she was only three years old, Heidi married Steven while he was attending law school. Stephen quickly noticed the warmth and affection that her family shared, but it wasn't until months after the wedding that Heidi's father, by then convinced that Stephen was a loving husband for his daughter, began letting barriers down and started to give his son-in-law a manly hug or other small sign of affection when they met or shared a warm moment with Heidi and her mother. "I was taken off guard, even after all that time," Stephen told me. "I knew full well that the simple things that got me so upset internally were nothing more than my father-in-law's perfectly natural way of telling me I was a member of the family. That's the way *he* was brought up. *I* was raised differently."

Robert had the opposite problem. Born into a family

quite masculine and are responding to the influence of a symbol well entrenched in the unconscious. Many men wear their hair long these days not because they particularly like it themselves, but because they've discovered that it stimulates *women.*

Every generation has its own antiestablishment, antiauthority way of dressing, grooming and acting. Very frequently, if enough people try to be *nonconforming,* the very means they take to achieve that goal becomes the *conforming* thing to do. Neither hair length, nor any other characteristic, indicates sexual preference. Homosexuals themselves are not attracted to any *one type* of man. Some like partners with long hair, others with short; some like men with smooth skin, others prefer bodies covered with hair. Some go for masculine-acting men, others are drawn to very effeminate partners. Variation is the same as when measured against the range of attraction of heterosexual men to women with blue or brown eyes, blond or brunette hair, big breasts, long legs and so on.

Another false indicator sometimes used to gauge the presence of homosexuality is a man's inability to be forceful; to stand up to his employer or to friends. Here again, this has absolutely nothing to do with homosexuality, but usually only stems from a poor sense of self-esteem. If a man has doubts about himself, he will have doubts about his ideas and he'll back down whenever he faces a more assured adversary. Many heterosexual men are incredibly *compliant* people, while many homosexual men are assertive, and aggressive.

FEAR OF HOMOSEXUALITY

Put into proper perspective, homosexuality is not quite the problem it might seem to be—at least not to homosexuals themselves. The *fear* of homosexuality is something else again, and poses a considerable problem for a great number of heterosexual men. Why else do comedians joke about it, playwrights invent laugh-provoking adventures around it, and young boys and men tease about it with an overdose of flipness and a heavy helping of cruelty? They do it because underneath the devil-may-care abandon, the sly and sometimes coarse humor, the lisps, exaggerated limp wrists and overly swaying hips, "straights" hide very real fears. Some get over it at a relatively early age, but for a great many men in this country, homosexuality poses a threat usually present under only minimal repression. The *fear* far outweighs *reality* but continues as an extremely prevalent concern in our male population. Many men will do anything they can to avoid giving anyone the impression that they are latent homosexuals.

Not all societies regard homosexuality with the same terror, of course. What to us may seem obscene or deviant has for centuries been viewed by some cultures in the Near East as acceptable and unworthy of mention or second thought. At the same time, what might seem appealing and quite normal to us—miniskirts, for instance—is considered perverse and immoral elsewhere.

But in our society men often compensate in terms of sexual bravado and so-called masculine pursuits in order to avoid even the slightest doubt from themselves and others that they are in any way tainted. It must be remembered that to many heterosexual men homosexuals are not male, not female, but a neuter gender devoid of any sexuality and without proper human identity at all.

There's an interesting sidelight to this point which I'd like to illustrate for a moment. You'd expect that a man, discovering his wife or girlfriend in a *lesbian* affair, would be angry and threatened by the presence of a third person in what should culturally be a strictly one-to-one, male-female relationship. Some men may react that way, but many don't equate female homosexuality with its male counterpart. They often do not take female sexuality seriously. Some men see it as nothing more than a prank of passing interest to the women involved and not something worth brooding over. Why? I believe that it is because these men think female sexuality is of itself so negligible that their lesbianism is also unimportant. The same type of man finds it much more difficult to cope with the discovery that his partner is engaged in a *heterosexual* relationship, because that constitutes "real" sexuality, unlike the "harmless" if annoying "playing around" of lesbianism. In the latter his male pride is, of course, hurt.

Heterosexual men, as we'll see, can dredge up latent fears of homosexuality in many ways and in many situations. A business reversal that injures a man's self-esteem may evoke homosexual fears. Childhood homosexual fantasies and homosexual incidents, however harmless and routine, can linger on, waiting for the opportune moment to come to the fore. Many men who suffer from impotence, for example, often confuse it with homosexuality, even though one may have nothing at all to do with the other. As studies have proven, homosexual men tend to be just as sexually aggressive and potent as their heterosexual counterparts. The objects of sexual and emotional excitation and devotion differ, but the intensity and "success-failure" interest is as powerful.

The fear of homosexuality is in large part a fear of helplessness and is equated with anything that is viewed as antimasculine. Calling oneself a homosexual in a self-derisive way (*e.g.*, in a dream or fantasy) is often a form of self-hate promoted by our culture which tells men that this is, in effect, one of the worst things to be. Of course the confusions, prejudices and misconceptions accumulated since childhood do not help.

MEN AND CHILDHOOD PRESSURE

Growing up, as we've already seen, is never easy. It is more difficult for an infant boy to assume his role of masculinity than for an infant girl to assume hers of femininity. Let me explain. With only rare exceptions, it's the mother who takes care of the children from infancy to adulthood, and no matter what efforts are made to counter the effect, little boys and little girls can't help but identify with mother and the feminine role.

For the young girl, the progression is smooth and direct. While she may have problems separating herself out as an individual different from her mother, she doesn't have to make a break in terms of sexual identification. The young boy, on the other hand, is faced with a greater task. Not only does he have to convince himself that he is an individual and therefore a separate person from his mother, he has to shift his sexual identity. Much research has been done in this area, and experts now believe that the boy must make the break and identify with his father, another male or masculinity in general by his *second* birthday. If the transition hasn't been made by that age, associations and identifications become harder to sort out and run the genuine risk of entrenching themselves even deeper as the years go by.

The changeover doesn't always take place. It is more difficult in a household with a domineering mother and a weak and virtually absent father—the most common combination that seems to be the best foundation for the development of a homosexual predilection. If, as I've mentioned before, the father can't be relied on and the mother is equated with strength, the young boy may then equate strength with femininity.

One way a youngster can make the necessary separation from mother—and our culture contributes to this distortion—is by creating the feeling that he is superior to women. By differentiating himself even more than needed, he can combat the dual fear of non-differentiation and the potential misidentification his mother's early care might have imposed on him. As long as he maintains this air of superiority—and it's a *lifelong* protection in most cases—he need never worry about slipping back to childhood vulnerability. To create this fictional self-image, he accepts or rejects any real differences that exist to his advantage and actually makes up new ones that don't exist on a *biological* level, but which he's pressured into believing on a *cultural* level. Physical strength, therefore, isn't enough in and of itself. Greater intelligence, superior judgment, and other less tangible but more important factors are added to the fictional mix. *Male chauvinism* and the *myth of masculinity* are the next steps in this kind of progression. Feelings and sensitivity aren't permitted to flourish within the confines of the myth, nor is weakness or fallibility, either on an emotional or logical plane.

FEAR OF DISCOVERY

It takes very little impetus for many heterosexual men to worry seriously about masculinity or the sort of manly impression they make on *other* people. But homosexual men and women continue to fear discovery, too. A recent study found that approximately *half* of all admittedly homosexual men and women are at one time or another afraid of being "discovered" by acquaintances. Women become less and less concerned with discovery as they enter middle age (the survey estimated that only ten percent remain fearful), while a substantial number of males (twenty-five percent) continue to worry.

DISPLAYING AFFECTION

As I've mentioned, fear—*real fear,* whether conscious or unconscious—very often dictates the things men do. As indicated earlier, the man who is afraid of doing anything that might be interpreted as homosexual makes every effort to behave in the most masculine manner. Perhaps one of the most obvious examples of this phenomenon appears in the command-suggestion little boys receive from their fathers: "You're a big boy now; you're a *man,* and *men* don't kiss other men; they shake hands! Show Uncle John what a *big man* you are and go over and give him a nice strong handshake!" By age seven or eight, this thinking is so ingrained in the boy that showing affection for other men (including his father) is extremely difficult. *Any* male-oriented affection has to be kept hidden. I know quite a few men who were deeply troubled by this and became *extremely* unhappy whenever they encountered a situation that posed the dilemma.

Stephen and Robert, who came from different parts of the country, shared *opposite yet identical* problems.

Stephen, a lawyer, had been raised in a Midwestern town by quiet parents who looked upon hard work and a rewarding good pat on the back as the ideal operative sequence of a man's life. In his family, women could kiss men, of course, and women could kiss other women (platonically on the cheek), but *no one dared even consider the possibility* that men could quite naturally greet each other with a hug or kiss on the cheek. When Stephen met Heidi, there was a conflict. Born in Switzerland and brought to the United States by her parents when she was only three years old, Heidi married Steven while he was attending law school. Stephen quickly noticed the warmth and affection that her family shared, but it wasn't until months after the wedding that Heidi's father, by then convinced that Stephen was a loving husband for his daughter, began letting barriers down and started to give his son-in-law a manly hug or other small sign of affection when they met or shared a warm moment with Heidi and her mother. "I was taken off guard, even after all that time," Stephen told me. "I knew full well that the simple things that got me so upset internally were nothing more than my father-in-law's perfectly natural way of telling me I was a member of the family. That's the way *he* was brought up. *I* was raised differently."

Robert had the opposite problem. Born into a family

of four brothers and three sisters, he was raised in a tradition that made masculine affection an ordinary, quite accepted part of life. Robert thought nothing of kissing his father and adult relatives and close friends when they met. When Robert got married, though, he joined a family where affection was reserved for the opposite sex—*only!* That meant that even tiny, unintentional indications of affection were taboo, including placing a hand on another man's arm to emphasize a point of conversation, or accidentally touching feet under the dinner table. Any sign that could in the *slightest* way be interpreted as sensitivity (much less as homosexuality) was forbidden and avoided at all costs.

Robert realized that his in-laws had themselves been raised in what he considered a puritanical tradition and were obviously convinced it was the proper way to behave, but he couldn't escape his gut feeling that they weren't *really* allowing him into their family and were withholding all but superficial affection.

I did explain to Stephen—and I reviewed with Robert—that male-to-male signs of affection are considered commonplace and perfectly heterosexual in many parts of the world. In Europe, the French and Italians, among others, greet one another with the traditional mock kiss on either cheek. In the Middle East, Arabs view similar greetings with the same innocence we feel when we shake hands or use the simple salutation *hello*. In Latin American countries, Brazil in particular, men greet other men with great bearhugs of affection, usually accompanied by happy and enthusiastic slaps on the back.

Obviously, comparisons weren't going to be very helpful to Stephen and Robert. How they and their in-laws behaved and reacted was neither the product of a few days of learning nor even a set of recently acquired habits. They did what they did because that's the way they had been taught from their earliest days.

Robert couldn't alter his in-laws' lifelong standards, but Stephen and I were able to analyze the whys and wherefores of his background as it contrasted with that of his wife's parents. Slowly, as he let himself realize that there weren't any threats to his masculinity and that his father-in-law wasn't betraying any subliminal leanings toward homosexuality, he relaxed and lowered the barriers part of the way. Although it still took him a long time to fully accept this new attitude, he did find that his outlook changed. He soon was able to enjoy visiting his in-laws from beginning to end, and not just in the middle between the welcomes and fare-wells.

Sometimes a simple defensive act of avoidance ex-tends into a more *offensive* sphere. I'm thinking par-ticularly of those men I've met who ward off any possibility of affection with a counterattack of com-petition and even friction. For most men, those options are preferable to the alternative of feeling affection, let alone showing it.

ATHLETICS AND MASCULINITY

Though men in their day-to-day lives are hesitant, if not hostile, to express affection between males, there is one area in which it is acceptable and even appropriate: the sporting event. Athletes not only do *not* refrain from signs of affection for one another, but actually demonstrate a great deal of it in front of a huge audience of fans.

Sports, interestingly, is one of the very few areas where men can reveal their more sensitive feelings. The next time you see a basketball game, watch closely after a player sinks a key shot or walks to the foul line. There's a good chance one of his teammates will pass by and give him a light tap on the backside as a sign of congratulations or reassurance. The same thing can be seen at baseball and football games, and hockey and soccer contestants routinely take this idea one step further. If a player scores a goal, teammates rush to his side and *hug him* with all the affection of men thanking someone who has just saved their lives. These players, who just a moment before were so rough and tough, can now lossen up a little and show affection. Chances are these same men would *never* be caught dead doing the same thing away from the arena or playing field, and certainly not in street clothes.

While we're at it, let's look at sports played by youngsters. Little League baseball games are chock full of pats on the backside, and junior hockey matches abound with hugs of delight. In this age of instant communication, television and the movies have made it possible for all young boys to seek out and emulate heroes. If a youngster sees his favorite ballplayer tugging at his left ear every time he makes a catch, the odds are pretty good that the idolizing youth will do the *identical* thing the next time he makes a catch in the neighborhood sandlot. The same holds true for pats, hugs and all the other seemingly non-macho displays, which shed all negative connotations as soon as the professionals are seen doing them before millions of onlookers.

MUSCLE MEN

There's another area worth discussing that may or may not be considered "sport," depending on one's point of view. In either case, the psychological implications demand attention. Magazine readers and former comic-book fans recall that skinny "ninety-pound weakling" whose girlfriend had to watch helplessly as a muscular bully kicked sand in his face. Every red-blooded boy who had ever been pushed around by the neighborhood roughneck or turned down for a date because of a somewhat underdeveloped physique empathized with that come-on for a popular body-building course. Some of those who filled out the coupon at the bottom of the page were looking forward to developing enough *strength* to actually fight off attackers, and many wished to develop *muscles* imposing enough to keep would-be villains away.

As every survey (and every man or woman with

whom I've discussed the subject) seems to agree, the improvement of *strength and endurance* is a *perfectly masculine endeavor*. To most of us, those attributes are considered both "normal" and practical. Even the gargantuan Olympic weight lifters are accepted by the general public as masculine, though many people find their contests boring or pointless. From a purely esthetic standpoint, weight lifters are usually not very appealing, either. Many have stomachs that appear as overdeveloped as the rest of their bodies.

The same doesn't hold true with regard to bodybuilders. A majority of men and women look askance at that preoccupation, wondering why the men who participate feel the need to bulge and bulge and bulge, and whether that form of bodily concentration doesn't really reflect adversely on a man's masculinity.

Well, *winning* in our culture is a universal goal. Some men may find it in a business triumph, and others merely in completing the Sunday crossword puzzle. The Mr. Universe and Mr. America contests aren't any different except that victory goes to the man who has created what the judges consider "the most perfectly developed body" among all the competitors.

Do the muscle magazines that crowd the racks at newsstands (right next to the girlie periodicals) really appeal to *heterosexual* men who simply want to *compete* in this area of rivalry—or to heterosexual men who can never hope to achieve qualifying proportions but enjoy the competition vicariously, much like baseball spectators? Or do they appeal to *homosexual* men who develop their bodies to attract other men or who buy the magazines for the erotic effect of the photographs? While it's always dangerous to generalize, studies have shown that a great many women are turned off by men with overly developed muscles, particularly when muscles have been enlarged to proportions that make the strongest-looking heavy-weight boxing champion seem a scarecrow in comparison.

In looking over the magazines myself, I've found that some are honestly directed toward a readership interested solely in the art of muscle development.

Some do appear designed to lure and appeal to men with *homosexual* preferences.

If the pictures *are* the seductive, languorous poses (by *male* instead of *female* models) that you'd find in any of the girlie magazines, there is reason for concern. Any young boy drawn to those publications should have some sort of professional consultation.

If, on the other hand, the pictures stress exercise, diet and proper muscle development, there is less reason for concern. The men with overdeveloped muscles are very probably coping with the problems of self-esteem and fear of dependency by creating their own sense of pride in a way they hope will be envied by others. Young boys whose bodies have not fully matured and whose sense of personal worth may be a bit shaky sometimes look to the men in the magazines as models to spur them on to the dedicated efforts required to build physical and mental self-esteem. There's more to be concerned about if the interest continues into adulthood. In those cases, the attention may be evidence of a severe lack of self-esteem and can even carry over into fears of unsatisfactory masculinity. In short, it may indicate a sense of inadequacy to one degree or another.

Joan and Nick were on the verge of marital collapse because of Nick's preoccupation with his physique. Joan, who at first had been attracted to him partially by his sturdy, hard body, was now concerned about his relative detachment and what she perceived as his narcissism. Nick's interest in himself manifested itself in ways that made him less than enthusiastic in everything he did with his wife, including sex. Exploring his past uncovered a clear history of diminishing self-esteem that eventually prompted him to compensate through body-building. His "selfish self-interest" had not yet developed by the time he married, but within several years both his body and his narcissism had grown to extraordinary proportions. Once he truly realized what he was doing and why, Nick was able to start the slow process of reevaluating his self-image as well as his relationship with his wife.

BISEXUALITY

No overview of homosexuality would be complete without a look at an area still not fully understood by the experts and even less so by the general public. Although others might disagree, I am in accord with those who feel that *bisexuals* are basically *homosexuals* attempting to make an adjustment on a heterosexual level. When we talk of bisexuals, of course, we aren't including children, who may well have passing homosexual experiences in the process of growing up, or adult men who may have a passing experience during military service or in prison. Those sorts of episodes are transient and shouldn't be considered in this context.

Earlier in this chapter, I touched on the problem of *homosexual* men who try to make a *heterosexual* adjustment but find that they occasionally have to go off and seek a homosexual encounter. Sporadic wanderers break down into four categories: (1) Homosexual men who *have* come to terms with their homosexuality; (2) Homosexual men who *have not* come to terms with their homosexuality but who nevertheless are driven compulsively; (3) Men who experiment with homosexuality but are not really homosexuals; and (4) the psychopathic or sociopathic man who has either weak or no moral standards and will try *anything* just because, like the mountain to the mountain climber, it's there and for "kicks." He may or may not be a homosexual.

The more difficult challenge often is not to the man coping with bisexuality, but to his *female partner* who must come to terms with his drives and efforts as they conflict with her own needs and vanity. A woman who enters a relationship, especially one of marriage, with a partner who is bisexual, is letting herself in for considerable difficulties. Without professional treatment, few, if any, bisexuals ever completely give up their homosexuality, and the success ratio isn't splendid even with the most sophisticated treatment. A woman whose lover is bisexual is in constant competition with his underlying homosexuality, whether or not he is actively seeking homosexual encounters. While his homosexuality remains an active force, she may be burdened with the feeling that *she* has the responsibility for keeping him heterosexually inclined. The pressures can be enormous, especially when we remember that most authorities feel homosexuality starts in the very early years of a boy's life. We're talking about a *core problem*, something that goes deep into the identifying substance of an individual.

Some women come to terms with the dilemma in what most people would consider surprising—even shocking—ways. I know of many women who allow their husbands to bring home a homosexual partner and who may—and this *does* happen—even go to bed with *both* men. Not quite as surprising is the fact that many bisexual men actually seek such an arrangement to relieve themselves of guilt feelings the crossover infidelity may evoke. "If my wife is participating," he reasons with himself, "she is condoning my activities." Needless to say, it isn't an easy or simple situation and often is fraught with many complications as well as a great deal of anxiety and despair.

Chapter 12

Sex (Body and Mind)

There is no greater nor keener pleasure
than that of bodily love—and none which
is more irrational.

—Plato, *The Republic*

Sex can be a source of much enjoyment and happiness. Whether or not it's the keenest of human pleasures is a question each of us must answer for himself, just as it must also be an individual decision as to how important a role sex will play in the overall scheme of life. Some people (particularly men) become obsessed with the quest for satisfaction to dominate them, while others regard sex as only one of many needs.

Sex may be an adjunct of compassion, full relating and sharing, but too many people carry on an endless search for warmth through purely sexual encounters. Needing to feel needed, loved, understood and together with another human being, they often mistake spasmodic coupling for love. From a purely *technical* viewpoint, the relief of sexual tension varies from person to person and can take place in many ways: heterosexually, homosexually, incestuously, sadistically, masochistically, by masturbation, with members of other species, with or without emotional involvement and through the use of any or all parts of the body and its orifices.

However it is practised, sex is seldom an entity in itself. It doesn't, after all, happen in a vacuum. Men, and women too, often utilize sex for reasons other than physical pleasure. And likewise, other seemingly non-sexual activities are sometimes sexual in meaning.

The relief of sexual tension is just *one of many areas* in which symbolic gratification can take place. Tad was enamored of large, powerful automobiles. He took great satisfaction in showing them off, and the faster he drove, the better he liked it. The louder the engine roared, the more powerful he felt. In the course of ensuing consultation, it became apparent that Tad had wrestled with serious self-doubts as he matured and that much insecurity undermined his masculine self-confidence. Somehow, the super-cars gave him the *sense of strength, assurance* and *macho* he felt he lacked.

Cars, of course, aren't the *only* sexual symbols. Guns often fill the same need as powerful automobiles. Sports and fighting release tensions in another way, and I think everyone knows about eating and talking —what more popular, readily accessible outlets for frustrations of all kinds are there? Dreams, both those that are obviously sexual and those that are sexually symbolic, also offer an alternative.

It happens that men (and some women, too) have quite a low anxiety tolerance, a trait that sometimes makes sex a kind of acceptable *sedative*. Because of that, sex can convey love—an ideal purpose—and ease tension too. It can quell anxious feelings, serve as a hypnotic, indicate support and closeness, and provoke enough fatigue to let sleep override any psychological pains troubling a person. Since it provides such wide-ranging side-effects, most men find it's better than popping a pill in times of anxiety and stress, and it's certainly more enjoyable. Some cardiologists say it's the best possible exercise, too.

COMPARTMENTALIZATION

Without getting technical, "compartmentalization" is the mental arrangement people use to subdivide their thoughts, memories and feelings into different value systems. One section may be reserved for business, another for family and another for something else. It's almost as if an internal computer system automatically evaluates the situation and determines which set of perceptions, values and actions should be adopted for the occasion.

Compartmentalization may be quite apparent in a man's attitude to sex. Since most women don't operate this way they can't understand how their partners can have a terrible fight with them one minute, then make love the very next minute—often without "making up."

"It's astounding," Mrs. V., the wife of a top-level management executive told me. "My husband and I argue from time to time, although that's not a particularly regular event. He does have enormous pressures at the office—pressures which he takes home with him and throws on my shoulders in a *most* unpleasant way. When we do have a fight or when he does come home all upset and seething about something at work, *I'm* certainly not in any mood to be sexual. If he wanted sympathy and cuddling that would be one thing. But he *doesn't*. He either wants to take out his aggressions through sex or he's somehow—I can't understand that at all—completely isolating his problems from our lovemaking."

In this particular case, I had to tell Mrs. V. that both were distinct possibilities. Men *do* use sex as a way of expressing rage and hostility, escaping from depression, enhancing self-esteem and all the other reasons already cited. Some use it as a means of keeping their distance from a partner or of avoiding the need to verbalize emotions (lovemaking can be silent or punctuated with sighs and moans, but neither partner is forced to utter words of endearment). Men can be angry (in one compartment) and loving (another compartment) and feeling sexual (still another compartment) and can tune out all other feelings while they have sex and tune back into other feelings after their sexual needs are taken care of.

Some women can't imagine, much less accept, that men can have a "purely" sexual experience with another woman—a "one-night stand," if you will—that includes *sex and only sex* without any emotional involvement. The feminist movement has started to change this outlook a bit, especially since more and more *women* are looking for sexual experiences that are not preludes to more meaningful relationships. Is the salesman really cheating if he sleeps with a woman he meets during a nine-week promotion tour far from his home and partner? Of course, he *is* cheating by secretly violating a written, oral or silent oath of fidelity, especially if at the same time he insists that his wife keep the contract. But is that quite the same as a man who consciously or subconsciously seeks deeper forms of *emotional involvement?*

The Don Juan Syndrome

With only the rarest of exceptions, the mechanics of lovemaking can be learned with study, repetition and guidance. With practice a man learns all the elements of *technique* and will even be able to *simulate* a kind of passion, but this isn't the same as making an *emotional investment*. To do that, he must care about his partner and must of course look at her as another full *human being* instead of as an exploitable object to be used for a short-lived physical experience. To do this he must be a "lover" and not only a mechanic. Genuine emoting, spontaneity and creativity in the service of lovemaking are seldom possible without genuine love.

The only way for a man to become a real lover is for him to feel at least some degree of emotional involvement with his partner. This involvement will motivate him to try to make her happy, and will help create a sense of mutual trust engendering in both an urge to be close and to "lose themselves in each other," during sexual intercourse.

The terms "mechanic" and "lover" aren't mutually exclusive, of course. A good lover may be a poor mechanic and vice versa, but many men *do* successfully combine the two possibilities. It is the lucky woman—and man—who enjoy a relationship characterized by love expressed ably through sex. Others who *don't* share this good fortune often must contend with arrangements that can prove dissatisfying at the least and downright unpleasant in the extreme cases. It's infinitely easier to teach the mechanics of sex than to attempt to provide absent sensitivity, feelings, caring and all else that comprises involvement on a deep emotional basis. Of course it is particularly difficult to make even initial inroads in a man who is very immature and full of macho confusions about so-called softer feelings. It must be remembered that an undeveloped infantile mentality is essentially a selfish one, which desires all kinds of feeding and knows little or nothing of sharing or giving.

MECHANICAL DIFFERENCES

The "mechanics" of sex (*i.e.*, the physical dos and don'ts) are obviously not to be ignored, for they are an integral part of any successful experience. Once a woman has deciphered many of her partner's *psychological* motivations, she still must discover which factors (both physical and psychological) permit him to *enjoy* actual sexual relations. For the most part, I'm not going to discuss the physical, although certain aspects go beyond the purely physical and enter the realm of psychology. They beg some mention.

As we've seen, men tend to become aroused more easily than women by superficial stimuli. There are also other major differences between the sexes but, as I've noted before, there are also a number of major similarities. The problem is, both sides tend to draw conclusions that aren't quite correct. Let me illustrate what I mean. Many erogenous zones and arousal signals are alike in men and women. Clearly a woman can't get an erection to the degree her partner can, but the clitoris does become hard when aroused. Depending on the circumstances, a woman's nipples will become erect if she is either sexually aroused or is physically cold. Sexual excitement may also raise a rash on a part of her body. The same things happen to men, particularly to their nipples, yet you *won't* find many men who concede that such similarities do exist. A percentage of men actually enjoy being touched and caressed on the nipples and in other places that would generally be considered "feminine" territory. They just back off from revealing these sensitivities out of fear that such "admissions" will betray feminine desires and therefore *threaten their masculinity*. At the same time, many women assume that because *women* enjoy having their nipples caressed, their partners do too. That assumption may be erroneous since many men find that any tactile attention paid to such zones is not only non-erotic, but distinctly irritating as well as threatening.

Kissing, of course, is a diverse marvel of its own. As a symbol of affection, it's the first step in lovemaking, but it may also serve as an indication of reward or merely of greeting. Some societies kiss with the lips, others with the cheeks and still others with noses. So the symbolism is there, *regardless* of the way it's expressed. It's not quite as clear whether all those forms of kissing also convey as much sensuality as does mouth-to-mouth affection in the Western world. Still, from a purely psychological standpoint, kissing does have its soothing aspects. After all, the suggestion to "kiss it and make it well" has proven to all of us at one time or another a worthwhile remedy. And it works for *adults* almost as well as for *children*.

MORE ABOUT ERECTIONS

Later on in this book, I'll discuss impotence, but here I'd like to clarify something that is misunderstood by many women. Despite thoughts to the contrary, the vast majority of men cannot "will" an erection. Yet I periodically hear women complain that their partner is intentionally *not* "willing" his penis into an erect state. The reason he isn't is that he *can't!*

The dynamics of arousal are always being studied, but it will probably be a long time before there is satisfactory comprehension of the intricate, subtle blending of the mind and body that takes place to produce an erection. We do know that men get aroused by various stimuli and that, at times, they *can avoid* erection by concentrating both visually and mentally on completely non-erotic subjects. As a result, there's some justification for believing that a man can keep himself from having an erection, although it is more difficult if the external or fantasy stimulus is sensual enough and/or if he hasn't found relief from sexual tension over an extended period of time. In that case, the *slightest stimulus* may be sufficient for arousal.

Only the rarest man can "will" his penis *into erection*. Most men can't do it. It either occurs spontaneously or with the help of the woman. But in this context, it is constructive for women to realize that a partner's inability to get an erection may have nothing at all to do with her, and is more often than not related to his own internal psychodynamics.*

Compartmentalization, I must add, does not mean that men can turn without *any* second thought to sex as an outlet during anxiety or depression. They can *turn* to it, but there's no guarantee they'll be able to attain and maintain an erection firm enough to have intercourse. In fact, intense anxiety, depression or fear act *negatively,* often making it impossible for the man to get an erection and, therefore, to use sex as an outlet.

SEXUAL POSITIONS: THEIR MEANINGS

Many people—and I think that *everyone* considers himself an amateur psychiatrist or psychologist from time to time—like to believe that the positions a couple take during sex tells much about them. If, for

* See next chapter for further discussion on impotence.

example, the woman is in the *superior* position (on top), then one interpretation may be that she is the *aggressor* and the *dominant* partner, while the man is the *follower* and the *weaker, more submissive* of the two. If the man's on top, then that interpretation can simply be reversed. I'm afraid that it doesn't sort out that easily, however. Positions *may* tell a trained analyst something about the participants' personalities, but only if the same position is assumed consistently and only—and most importantly—if the analyst knows a *great deal* about his subjects before attempting to draw conclusions. Snap judgments *don't* work. A good percentage of men like variety and do vary positions, but there are many other men who find a particular position easier than the others and more satisfying to both partners.

Despite what all the sex manuals suggest, altering positions doesn't provide a great deal of heightened physical thrills. Changes are *psychological* and it's the variety and difference in approach that add to eroticism. Men like change now and then because it offers a challenge and a new outlook (literally and figuratively).

Anal intercourse (where entry is made through the anus and not the vagina) is usually initiated by men out of *curiosity*. Some experts, however, believe that men who are interested in a woman's buttocks and who consistently seek to enter her from the rear are responding to a desire to mount her and to possess her in an aggressive, even sadistic manner. Other motives include the potential tightness and control the position promises and, sometimes to a certain subconscious degree, hostility and even sadism. Even the crude expression to "get it up the ass" has cultural implications symbolic of anger, mastery, exploitation and conquest. This interpretation holds true for anal intercourse for some people. In any case, if anal intercourse is attempted, it must be done with care, because it can lead to urethral infection in the male and to tearing of the vital anal sphincter muscle in the woman. Neither is a pleasant possibility.

Many men and women believe that they are not enjoying sex to the fullest unless they succeed in having *simultaneous* orgasms. Under those conditions, much pressure falls on the man, who must sustain his erection—*without ejaculating*—until his partner starts to experience an orgasm of her own. Simultaneous orgasm may have its proponents, but there's absolutely nothing "wrong" with serial orgasms. The serial method allows both partners to focus on each other's pleasure without the overwhelming distraction of their own sensations and needs. While the man still has to wait for his partner, he is relieved of the burden of waiting until the precise moment she hits her peak. Women who are non-orgasmic or who have the capacity for many orgasms can be helpful in considering their partners' endurance and needs.

Closed eyes during lovemaking sometimes pose another relatively minor problem. "If he/she really loves me, why doesn't he/she keep his/her eyes open and look at me? Is he/she really thinking about someone else?" The answer breaks down into several parts. Closing the eyes may stem simply from the mistaken belief that keeping one's eyes open is a crass and primitive thing to do during such a magic moment. More likely, it has to do with a fear that one set of open eyes will meet the other set of open eyes and the result will be an aura-destroying, comic meeting of crossed eyes. Some individuals who close their eyes may be trying to get in touch with themselves *while* becoming lost in the sensuality and overpowering emotional and physical electricity of the moment. Sex is also, in its way, a very selfish and self-indulgent kind of activity. Although two people are taking part, each is experiencing his or her own sensations and wants to make the most of them (even while desirous of satisfying the partner). Some people, both men and women, are made to feel *guilty* about having a pre-occupation with pure abandon and enjoyment, despite the reality that precisely that attitude is perfectly "normal" and *very* human.

Chapter 13

Sexual Problems

My body, which my dungeon is,
And yet my parks and palaces.
—Robert Louis Stevenson,
"To a Gardner"

Sexual problems abound, and they range from relatively mild disturbances in function to chronic inability to engage in sex on any level. While numerous books have been written by experts in the field, too many of them focus on miseducation as the main cause of difficulty. Poor sexual information, confusion and nonconstructive practices do play a role, but the most serious cause of difficulties are usually emotional in origin.

Impotence, a common and extremely demoralizing problem, can manifest itself in several ways, including total inability to achieve an erection or the loss of an erection once insertion is attempted or takes place. The experience itself may generate enough anxiety to perpetuate the condition and repeated attacks of impotence continue to produce a self-fulfilling prophecy. Of course impotence often prompts concern about masculinity as well as fear of physical decline. In chronic impotence a man may suffer from considerable self-hate and depression, feelings which make sexual competence even more difficult to achieve, thus completing a vicious cycle. In an effort to relieve themselves of self-hate, some men displace their hostility (and responsibility for the condition) on their wives. This can further complicate and sometimes destroy a sexual relationship. The woman may at the same time begin to feel rejected, or may interpret the man's "failure" as an indication of her inability to arouse him. One thing works on another until both partners are entangled in a complicated and unhappy relationship that often extends beyond the sexual area of their lives.

PHYSICAL CAUSES OF IMPOTENCE

In discussing impotence, it is vital to realize that most troubles stem from psychological causes and not from physical difficulties. There are, however, on rare occasions physical causes, which I would like to touch on briefly. The most common example is the impotence some men suffer as a result of drinking too much alcohol. Of course, the tolerance level for one man will not necessarily be the same for another. While one can down the equivalent of ten shots of whisky without any appreciable change in behavior patterns or abilities, another needs only one scotch and soda to suffer the effects of alcohol. Depending on the user, alcohol may sometimes serve as a stimulant or as a relaxant (or a paralyzer if taken to excess), but this, too, is contingent on the individual's constitution and the amount of liquor consumed. The same is true for various drugs, whether hard, soft or prescription. It all depends on who, what and how much.

Starvation or improper diet can cause impotence by upsetting the body's circuitry and draining it of energy, and any type of deep fatigue (hard work, exercise, emotional drain) can also be a factor. The body's intricate system may also be upset by a number of internal problems, including infections, severe diabetes and arteriosclerosis. Still, physically-caused impotence is relatively unusual, and where the cause is not reasonably obvious, a medical checkup should be arranged.

IMPOTENCE OF EMOTIONAL ORIGIN

Every man experiences some impotence temporarily sooner or later. It can be engendered by the mere fear of impotence; a perfectly "normal" man may be so frightened by the thought that he will inadvertently *bring it on himself*.

Initial sexual experiences are often frightening to young men worried about "performing" successfully. Much of the fun and joy of sex is replaced by anxiety sufficient to cause transient inability to maintain an erection. Some men get over their anxiety without undue repercussions. Others unfortunately are sufficiently traumatized to establish a chronic problem.

Today's mores have altered our outlook as to what constitutes a "proper" age for sexual initiation, but there still are some men whose initial full sexual experience takes place on the wedding night. As the center of attraction of friends and relatives during the wedding ceremony and celebration, as the "victim" of knowing smiles and leers, it is not inconceivable that the groom feels pressured to perform, to uphold the honor of "all men" the first time he has sex with his wife. This is a situation that can be thoroughly traumatizing and terrorizing psychologically—one that can lead to temporary impotence.

There are some men who have no problems at all with sex *before* marriage, but who start to suffer dysfunction *after* marriage. These are sometimes men who feel trapped by a legalized union and its ensuing responsibilities, and who cannot tolerate the intimacy that marriage connotes. Other men once married become temporarily impotent because they feel threatened by the possibility of parenthood.

The fear of aging is another emotional problem that can wreak havoc on the mind and the body of even the youngest and most potent of men, as can misinformation about a hernia or diseases of the urinary system, prostate or genitals.

Emotional depression, whatever its origin, may cause impotence. The same is true of severe anxiety.

SURGERY: THE FACTS

Prostate surgery rarely produces physical cause for impotence. However it can be psychologically traumatic and may produce impotence on an emotional basis. Situated near the base of the bladder, the prostate plays an important part in the process of reproduction. The prostate gland produces the fluid that eventually conveys the sperm to the egg. The gland becomes engorged with sexual excitation, and unless semen is discharged, pain in the groin sometimes ensues. In middle age some men suffer chronic benign enlargement of the prostate gland, which can impair urinary function, making prostatectomy (removal) necessary. Once this is done, ejaculation of semen is no longer possible, even though the man can go on having orgasms and penile contractions. Of course this precludes fertilization, but while the man is no longer virile (cannot fertilize a woman's egg) he continues to be potent (able to have erections and intercourse).

Any number of factors can cause acute *prostatitis,* an infection that can occur in men of any age. Fortunately, it responds well to antibiotics and other medications. *Chronic prostatitis,* which is more difficult to cure, lasts longer and may recur. It, too, can be overcome.

More terrifying, of course, is cancer of the prostate. It's a disease that usually occurs in older age and is therefore seen more frequently as men live longer. If caught early enough, cure is possible, but chances diminish greatly once the cancer has spread to other parts of the body. Interestingly, *one* means of controlling the malignancy is to introduce female hormones into the man's body at the same time that the male hormone-producing testicles are removed. Quite bluntly, that's castration. Should we be surprised, then, when men afflicted by *any* type of prostate problem feel a dual threat to their lives *and* their masculinity? Fortunately only a small percentage of patients with prostate difficulties require or receive such radical treatment.

But what about the psychological impact? Trauma can often be severe. Many men cannot throw off their conviction that once cured, prostate problems— even those that don't lead to castration—impede sexual fulfillment. There is usually no physical correlation between erection and prostate difficulties, but unfortunately there is a psychological correlation.

Cystoscopy, an examination of the bladder that requires insertion of a tube into the opening in the penis and up through the urethra, can cause fears equally paralyzing. In such cases, the penis is *directly* involved, heightening the threat to the all-important symbol of maleness and that maleness connotes in our society.

CHRONIC EMOTIONAL IMPOTENCE

While temporary impotence is a severe and terrifying problem (almost always due to an acute attack on self-esteem such as losing a job or failing an exam), it *is* temporary. Understanding the cause and seeking a solution will usually eliminate it. Chronic impotence is another matter. It is potentially overwhelming and can be most destructive to the self-esteem and well-being of the man it afflicts. Chronic impotence is, by definition, a continuing and long-term condition and often has roots in relatively early life. It can be extremely difficult to remedy.

Parents can unwittingly nudge a son toward eventual impotence by being overprotective, inhuman, overly strict, or by stressing the *negative aspects* of both *sex and pleasure* in general. A mother who is exploitative and provokes incestuous feelings, or who is clinging and highly manipulative while her husband is passive, can

116

prompt impotence. So can parents who raise a young-ster in a household devoid of personal and emotional feelings, or who stress sex education that is basically antiwoman.

Lewis, thirty-seven, was plagued by chronic impo-tence from the very start of his adult sexual experience. He had no trouble realizing that the origins of his prob-lem could be traced back to his family situation. By consistently belittling him, his parents had failed to make him fully appreciate himself. Fortunately, Lewis had excellent motivation and eventually developed in-sights which helped immeasurably.

Another patient, William, suffered from impotence prompted by a variation of Lewis's childhood situation. William received little moral support from his father, a frustrated high school basketball player who had never gone to college and whose second-level talent had led him to be rejected numerous times by the various semipro teams he sought to join. At the same time that his father refrained from instilling confidence, he pushed William to strive to be a better basketball player than the youngster could *ever* hope to be—or want to be, for that matter. The father pushed and pushed, all the while competing with his son and trying his best to beat him every time they got on the backyard basketball court. William received an athletic scholarship to college, then dropped out of school his first year and joined the Merchant Marine. He was mixed up, beaten down and impotent, but he finally got away from his father and the direct need to fulfill all of his father's own failed expectations. He was only cured, however, after much struggle with his own values and standards and the raising of his self-esteem.

Chronic impotence may also result from traumatic sexual experiences in early life (these include incest, rape or various non-coital humiliations). A background of emotional disturbance can precipitate impotence too.

Despite what some doctors say, by the way, *frigidity* in a woman cannot really be equated with impotence. Although the psychology of men and women *is* similar in many ways, and both partners may react in similar fashion to the presence or absence of physical excitation, a frigid woman can almost always have intercourse; an impotent man cannot. If the female partner is not aroused sufficiently to allow her to enjoy orgasm, she usually can *at least take part*. In many cases, a woman who is frigid and who loves her partner will do her best to satisfy him, even if that effort includes intercourse without orgasm on her part. But, of course, consultation with a competent sex therapist is indicated, so that she may fully enjoy satisfaction. This almost always involves treatment and cooperation of both partners.

PREMATURE EJACULATION

The definition of premature ejaculation is still open to controversy. Masters and Johnson, in *Human Sexual Inadequacy,* consider it an ejaculation that takes place before one's partner is satisfied, whether prior to insertion or during actual intercourse. However, as I noted earlier, it is the rare man indeed who can withstand vigorous stimulation over a very long period of time, regardless of how great his desire to satisfy his partner. Also, the more a man fears premature ejaculation, the *more likely he is to experience it,* because the tendency to ejaculate prematurely is directly proportional to the amount of anxiety that is present. If a man has been experiencing premature ejaculation as an offshoot of his fears about being a good lover, for example, then his problem is only going to get worse as he becomes increasingly tense and anxious each succeeding time he tries anew to be a successful lover and then fails by ejaculating too early.

From the perspective of nature and history, it seems altogether possible that quick ejaculation was *an asset* during primitive times. Early man lived a life replete with dangers, and he was neither refined enough nor had sufficient time to enjoy lovemaking of extended duration. In the prehistoric era, intercourse was probably used primarily for fertilization, though it was, we may suppose, still enjoyable. Fast fertilization was probably of prime importance in a species vulnerable to many kinds of sudden attack.

In some instances premature ejaculation reflects *more* than mere anxiety. There are some men who harbor hostility toward women and demonstrate their antipathy by teasing them and keeping them in a state of frustration. Other men will ejaculate too quickly out of fear of involvement. If they can avoid a unified sexual experience, they conclude, they can—and are—avoiding the possibility that they'll have to face the threat of any emotional demands. Both of these psychodynamic motives usually go on unconsciously. Extremely potent men may occasionally have the problem, as may young boys at the height of their sexual prowess who are influenced by youthful impatience, eagerness and inexperience.

Premature ejaculation can often be eradicated by consultation with a competent sex therapist coupled with appropriate education and a prescribed regime of sexual exercises consisting of repeated practice in sexual activity. If this doesn't work, psychiatric intervention may be necessary to cope with underlying psychological problems.

The "waiting" period (waiting for the female partner to be satisfied) can however, be prolonged unreasonably. "Limits" must not exceed human possibility lest considerable misery ensue. One couple came to see me complaining that the husband's premature ejaculation was ruining their marriage. There was absolutely no dispute about the problem and the man agreed with his wife that *he* was clearly responsible for their difficulty. They had contacted me after talking over the situation and deciding that therapy for the man would be worthwhile, no matter how long it took. It soon became obvious that the wife had a problem, too. She was unable to be satisfied until they had had intercourse for almost an hour without stop. What to them was *premature ejaculation* was, in reality, a display of monumental sexual *stamina* by the husband.

In this case, the immediate problem was easily solved by instruction regarding ample clitoral stimulation.

The cure for premature ejaculation depends on the individual, of course. If overexcitation is the core problem, then more frequent intercourse and/or masturbation is sometimes the answer. Masters and Johnson have also described a technique of squeezing the penis that has proven helpful in stopping the ejaculatory process. Repeating this process produces desensitization, and each successful experience adds confidence and dilutes the problem. But it is better for a couple to have the guidance of a professional in undertaking this kind of program.

RARITIES

There are men who have trouble having ejaculations *at all*. In this case, what may start out as highly satisfying for the woman eventually turns to a sense of rejection. Her partner, who may find it difficult to give of himself in general, has a powerful psychological block against "letting go" during lovemaking. This is a problem which sex therapists find more difficult to remedy because it almost always involves the entire personality, rather than miseducation or poor experience. These men often require psychoanalytic treatment and adjunct sex therapy.

Even more unusual is *priapism,* a condition that provides a man with a continuous erection. This problem, *urological* and not psychological in origin, may produce considerable pain and is often associated with little or no sexual desire.

Chapter 14

Fantasies

Imagination is more important than knowledge.
  —Albert Einstein, *On Science*

The mind is the most complicated entity on earth and, in a way, may be viewed as comprising the sum total of ourselves and our existence. It may also be viewed as a kind of passionate tape recorder. It is additionally capable of great flights of imagination and fancy. It has the ability to make fantastic and exotic journeys in dreams while we sleep, and through fantasies when we are awake. Our dreams are less controllable than our fantasies and spring from our unconscious minds. Indeed Freud called dreams "the royal road to the unconscious," since proper analysis of a dream reveals much about ourselves of which we are usually unaware.

Fantasies are somewhat different because we can produce them at will. If we desire, in fantasy we can decide where we're going to go, what we're going to do, whom we're going to meet and when we're going to bid them all good-bye. It's as though a film is being shown within the mind, and we have written the script *our* way, selected *our* favorite cast with *ourselves* in the starring role, having designed the scenery, composed the background music and designated all the other factors that go into a successful entertainment venture. As producer and director, we can improve performances, praise people we like, humiliate those we can't stand and literally have *everything* the way *we* want it.

There's nothing *wrong* with fantasies themselves, no matter what the fantasy is. As long as fantasizing doesn't get out of control by distorting one's approach to real life, it is not ordinarily a destructive activity. Virtually everyone fantasizes—in large doses and in bits and pieces. It is so common an activity that, like breathing, we often hardly realize our minds have drifted off into fantasy. While some fantasies are fragmentary, and once gone are gone virtually forever, others are long and full of the substance of our lives. Many people retain lifelong fantasies to which they return again and again.

Some fantasies are emotional, some intellectual, some well thought out, some spur-of-the-moment and seemingly unrelated to what is *actually* occurring. Some fantasies are anesthetizing, while others produce outrage, tears, even hysteria. The important thing is that *all* fantasies have meanings, but, like dreams, few are easily interpreted. Many require an in-depth knowledge of the individual involved, and even then the best trained psychoanalysts need years to learn the meanings of symbols used by a particular person during fantasy journeys.

Some few fantasies, on the other hand, are obvious. In any event, they serve many purposes and are not, of course, the exclusive domain of men. Fantasies may provide escape from unpleasantness in a person's current environment or help in the resolution of a special problem or conflict. They may serve to stimulate or to repress an emerging feeling. As a private drama, they can be the proving ground for desires and emotions too frightening to be expressed overtly. Or fantasies may be rehearsals for some activity that will, indeed, eventually be translated into reality.

Many men are *terrified* by fantasies, largely because they apply the same values, standards and judgments to them as they do to real life and actual action, and because they are unable to understand what the daydreams indicate. Given the complexities of the human mind, it's no wonder the mental scenarios can run the gamut from wonderful to cruel and bizarre. Children frequently have wide-ranging fantasies, recollection of which may later torture them as adults.

TYPES OF SEX FANTASIES

While fantasies take many shapes and can involve every conceivable topic, the focus turns easily to sexual fantasies. Most people have them every day—often *several* times a day, and at times on and off all day long—and these, too, in most cases, are perfectly normal. They fall into the three broad categories: (1) those that are *overtly sexual* and truly born of sexual feelings, needs and desires; (2) those that seem non-sexual on the surface but are sexual on a deeper level. These frequently occur in the minds of people who attempt to repress their sexual feelings. For example, a man constantly picturing himself walking into houses and deep tunnels may well be camouflaging thoughts of intercourse; (3) those that are overtly sexual but are cover-up nonsexual, hidden feelings. A man who harbors repressed feelings of rage and vindictive triumph, for instance, may have sadistic sexual fantasies. None of this is unusual once we realize that we express much of ourselves through our sexual likes and dislikes. Sex itself is highly symbolic of the manner in which we encounter life in general. Men who are very aggressive and indifferent to their partners' needs—and are even cruel and selfish in bed—may subconsciously, and consciously too, fear and even *hate* women.

We can't escape the reality that there is still a high degree of repression in most societies today. When the feelings and desires of men (and women) are ignored and repressed, they often result in wildly exaggerated fantasy productions. The very society that maintains the strongest restrictions ultimately creates fantasies that are laden with the substance most tabooed by that particular society. The cartoon that shows a man in a nudist colony wishing that he could see the young lady in front of him with her clothes *on* instead of *off* is an example. In Saudi Arabia, where women are severely restricted in their social activities and where many still hide their faces behind veils, it is very probable that many men share fantasies of women seen *without* their veils. Similarly, a young man raised in a part of the world where sexual contact with women of other nationalities is frowned upon may invent a secret world in which he consummates one torrid affair after another with precisely these "forbidden" women.

ORIGIN AND PURPOSE

As I already noted, there's really no limit to the subject matter that can go into a fantasy. Imagination is without boundaries and fantasies are wide-ranging. But into what categories do most of these daydreams fall and why? Here each can be taken as a separate entity or combined with others, depending on the individual in question. First, let's not forget that *sexual fantasies* are *normal* and may well serve as a method of keeping human beings primed for procreation. But obviously they exist for other reasons as well.

Many men use sexual fantasies to increase their general sense of aliveness, creating highly romantic illusions that can partially compensate for sex lives that may be relatively boring, mundane or lacking in warmth or expression. This isn't only true sexually, as many of us have discovered at one time or another. Anyone who is trapped in a particularly boring job or a job that doesn't require mental dexterity probably fantasizes quite often. These excursions don't *necessarily* have to involve sex, though. They may focus on another job or some mythical scenario—anything that will take the fantasizer away from the humdrum present in which he finds himself.

Men's *sadistic* and *masochistic fantasies* are quite common, and are sometimes the result of repressed

124

rage either at others or at themselves. A man who feels unhappy with something he did, who has unresolved past conflicts, or who feels inadequate in general is particularly prone to masochistic daydreams. Some men have been overwhelmed and inundated by the necessity to be nice, clean and pure, and in fantasy have themselves wallow in symbolic or literal filth. It's an attempt at a paradoxical cleansing process. The sadistic and masochistic fantasies serve to bring the man (who has always been "nice, clean and pure") down to human levels and allow him to feel cleansed of pride in purity which has blocked sexual feelings. They may also permit a man with low self-esteem to manipulate or to dominate his real-life oppressors.

Anticonventional fantasies are often used to express rebellion against internalized parental authority or powerful, paralyzing religious scruples.

Both *heterosexual* and *homosexual fantasies* are experienced by men (and women) who are afraid to feel warmth and express actual closeness to *either* sex.

Serial-like fantasies are popular with extremely lonely men who live with certain characters from day to day just as if the dreamer was writing a continuing television soap opera. I have known men who maintained their own personal scenery and casts inside their heads. Each of the men had developed complicated plots with subplots and sub-subplots, and kept the stories progressing neatly each time he thought about them. These continuing adventures differ from repeated fantasies in which men return again and again to the same scene and review the same action and dialogue. Often these ongoing fantasies are repeated because they are especially stimulating or enjoyable as escapist fare.

Stimulating fantasies can also be used to satisfy yearnings for forbidden childhood desires (incest, to cite one).

Fantasies of sex with complete strangers sometimes stem from boredom or a resentment of family or work responsibilities. In effect, this kind of fantasy is a substitute for getting away from the "everyday" routine.

Fantasies of sex with younger women can arouse feelings of youth and memories of actual past encounters.

Of course variations on all of these categories are enormous. The meaning, as I indicated before, is seldom apparent, and fantasies are actually only "crazy," awful or bizarre if we apply *conventional value judgments* to them. In most circumstances, they are harmless and sometimes serve to help people feel momentarily better. But human compassion, as well as scientific, objective observation, is needed in order for an expert—much less a wife or girlfriend—to evaluate what a man's fantasies may mean in terms of a couple's short and long-range relationship.

Many fantasies are born during early adolescence or puberty when there's a good deal of frustration. The fantasies, as a result, tend to be *very powerful* and are often linked to voyeuristic tendencies. The boy develops a strong desire to *see,* whether it's pornographic literature, films or the real thing. These are the fantasies, modified or unaltered, that often stay on as he becomes a man and go on to become a stimulating device in his adult life.

MALE AND FEMALE FANTASIES ARE NOT THE SAME

Since every woman has fantasies of her own, and since a great deal of the foregoing could apply to them as well as to men, some women may assume that there is little if any difference between male and female daydreams. Subject matter varies of course, but in overall design and style, they do tend to be similar. But there are also some revealing differences. According to a number of studies, it has been demonstrated that men have numerically *more* sexual fantasies than women. At the same time, men's fantasies are usually simpler and lack the *subtlety and romanticism* of the female counterparts. A man, for example, will call upon his imagination to create a woman of ultimate sensuality: the "perfect" sexual object, endowed with whatever physical traits most excite him. If he desires it, he may have her do something he considers especially erotic, and these actions can range from merely walking to every type of activity, sexual or otherwise. The woman of this man's dream may have a recognizable face—she may be someone he knows or has seen in real life—or she may have a face he idealizes. In many instances, the woman is given *no face at all* since that key element to her personality may not be required.

Women can also have fantasies of pure sexual or social intercourse, or a combination of the two. But when they create a sexually attractive man, they usually want him to have a face. More than that, many women want him to have a distinct personality *and* they want a story, no matter how vague, to put the hero into context. Where a male may simply think of making love to a sexy woman, a female may think of herself as a princess with her fantasy prince carrying her off. She may establish a more romantic mood generally and fill in more of life's details, creating a sexual panorama in which the act itself plays only a small part. This is not always true, however, and there are many people of both sexes who have fantasies which are indistinguishable in terms of male or female identity.

FANTASIZING: ITS COMPLICATIONS

I said before that there are no limits to the subject matter of fantasies. However, just as a man may have some control about what can go into a daydream, he may also have some control about what stays *out*. I say "some control" because there are fantasies that are direct products of the unconscious, some of which come up compulsively again and again, and over which we may have no control at all. These, however, may be attempts we are making to let ourselves in on feelings we have attempted to hide from ourselves, and as such can be valuable in conveying self-information. But even fantasies that we consciously initiate and sustain almost always, like dreams, have at least some unconscious roots and motives.

Jacques was convinced that his wife deserved his entire devotion. There is nothing extraordinary about a sense of intense loyalty to a partner, only *his* loyalty went beyond even the most ardent of passions. To Jacques, only absolute purity could be tolerated in the relationship. He had convinced himself that he had *no right* whatsoever even to look at any other woman. To make the restrictions even more stringent, he had persuaded himself that not even the smallest association, however imaginary and fleeting, was allowable. If he *looked* at another woman he felt guilty, and if he ever *thought* of another woman while he made love to his wife, he castigated himself for days afterward.

Fortunately, most men aren't hamstrung like Jacques. Many feel good and enjoy life—and fantasies too— because they are freer, don't have Jacques's overbearing conscience, and aren't forever struggling to reach some elusive, impossible ideal of purity and morality. They aren't trying to achieve a unique oneness with their mates which essentially creates a two-headed monster instead of sustaining a healthy state of cooperative but individual identities. They see marriage realistically, not as two people fusing into one and riding off into the sunset, but as a *partnership* between two individuals, each different and special in his and her own way. They don't suffer from unusual guilt because they aren't always striving for an unattainable goal, and don't punish themselves for falling short of it, as well as for other imagined wrongs.

Fantasy of another woman can be stimulating, but also can have a meaning *beyond sex:* such a fantasy sometimes signifies infidelity and rebellion against *all kinds of contractual agreements and conventions.* The fantasizer is rebelling against society and the imposition of rules, and through rebellion he experiences a liberating effect, however short or synthetic.

The opportunity to be with more than one woman

at a time (even if it is totally imaginary) satisfies male curiosity and sets the stage for an interesting and erotic experience. It brings the man as close as he can *safely* come to the reality of sexual contact with another woman.

The possibility of escaping even momentarily the feeling of entrapment enables a man to reduce the tension of an exclusive commitment. Tension and anxiety in this regard are especially prevalent in men who are detached and who have regarded freedom from emotional involvement as the mainstay of feeling safe and secure. For these men any dilution of closeness, even in fantasy, is relieving. I may point out here that a detached man may also be a highly puritanical man and may also harbor fantasies of great closeness and even oneness. Obviously these diverse drives may make for considerable unconscious conflict and for actions on a conscious level (running to and then away from one's lover and being alternately sexually ardent and then cold) that may be confusing to both the man himself and his mate.

In the majority of instances, the "other woman" fantasy involves what might be considered by most people fairly "normal" sex. There isn't a large percentage of men who design fantasies in which they put their penises in a woman's ear or watch as she makes love to a gorilla. Sadism and masochism are more common ingredients, however, for reasons noted earlier in this chapter. One very popular fantasy has the woman tied up or chained so that she is totally unable to resist the fantasizer's sexual advances. She struggles, tugging and squirming with all her might to break free, but *no matter how hard she tries,* she fails and is forced to have intercourse with the fantasizer. Later, having barely recovered from the violent rape, she realizes what an *incredibly good lover* he was and what she would be missing if she didn't avail herself of such a marvelous opportunity. Now, rather than fight him off, she becomes completely compliant, *begging* him to make love to her. The fantasizer has won. His sexual prowess has conquered the most resistant, sexy woman imaginable. Of course she is only imagined, and most men who have this fantasy, when asked if they would find it stimulating to actually act it out, indicate that not only would they *not want* to do so, but they would also be generally repulsed by such behavior.

While this fantasy has a sadistic element, at the same time it includes great visions of glory. It is not uncommonly found in men who somehow are frightened by women. They find fantasies in which they restrict and control women temporarily supportive in easing their fear. There are a few men who really *do* practice bondage and sadomasochism with their wives, girl friends and prostitutes, but there is a wide chasm between fantasy and reality. Few men take the leap.

Ordinarily, fantasies are harmless, but if they become total substitutes for real living, they produce much self-deprivation. Viewing our fantasies with derision and contempt produces self-hate and has a demoralizing effect. Viewing them as creative expressions and extensions of ourselves leads to increased self-acceptance and can help increase self-understanding.

Chapter 15

Masturbation

> Often have I sighed to measure
> By myself a lonely pleasure
> Sighed to think, I read a book
> Only read, perhaps by me.
> —William Wordsworth,
>   "To the Small Celandine"

"*Normal* boys don't do that!"
  "Do you want it to fall off?"
  "You'll go blind if you keep on doing that!"
  "That's disgusting!"
  "That's sick!"
  "That's dirty!"

If we came across these emphatic statements without knowing what they were about, we would interpret them as descriptions of a perverse activity. And this is true as far as many people are concerned. To a large number of men and women, masturbation *is* perverted, destructive, lewd and immoral.

Even in our fairly liberated society, even with wide dissemination of information on masturbation, an incredible number of adults frown on the activity. Yet masturbation is healthy and not injurious. It relieves tensions, heightens sexual sensitivity and gives pleasure. And though it is difficult for those people who are sexually inhibited or tethered by a sense of Victorian morality to admit, virtually every adult male has masturbated during his lifetime. Masturbation is an activity so universal and so accepted by every range of medical authority that many experts now regard men with no history of masturbation as probably having serious emotional and sexual problems.

131

Earlier we discussed the long-range, corrosive guilt that can be engendered by boyhood misinformation regarding masturbation. If this book can help parents or prospective parents avoid that trauma for their children, it will be a wonderful bonus. I only hope to show that masturbation is perfectly normal and that men need not have anxieties about past episodes.

Again, I must reiterate: masturbation will not make the penis fall off; it won't cause blindness, acne, insanity, paralysis, senility, sterility or any of the other five-hundred assorted plagues some people give it credit for. It is not a *sick* thing to do, and it's not "dirty" in the sense of being lewd.

Another fallacy concerning masturbation is that it causes or indicates homosexuality. According to one line of reasoning, any man who masturbates is homosexual because he is involved with *himself* rather than with a member of the opposite sex. Most men will choose to have intercourse without any hesitation if they have the option. But even men who prefer masturbation have no special predilection for homosexuality. When they masturbate, heterosexual men usually engage in heterosexual fantasies, although homosexual ones sometimes occur too.

The main problem involving masturbation is not the act itself, but the guilt that is often engendered by the individual who is either ill-informed, a victim of social conditioning, or both.

A few years ago I had in therapy a soft-spoken, gentle young man in his early twenties. Frank was raised in a strict, orthodox Catholic family and was totally terrified by masturbation. He would eagerly have done almost anything rather than face more of the psychological punishment he was undergoing. Yet he still masturbated frequently, and the more upset he became, the more he masturbated. Masturbation relieved the anxiety . . . temporarily. Then the fear returned and shifted to anxiety. Anxiety prompted masturbation and the vicious cycle churned on like a perpetual-motion machine.

Frank's guilt, anxiety and terror were complicated by his religion. Each time he went to confession, which he did regularly, he listed what he felt were sins to a priest whom he could not see in the confessional. Masturbation is a sin to the Catholic church, so each time he confessed, promising to try to avoid a repetition of his sins, he was given penance (consisting of repeated prayers). Each time he confessed, he sensed that his confessor was becoming more annoyed because he displayed no progress in curtailing his masturbatory activities. Although Frank didn't mind the penance—after all, he was certain that masturbation was so wrong that no punishment was strong enough to wash away his guilt—he was increasingly upset by his confessor's displeasure.

I did not want to influence Frank either to decrease his masturbation nor to formulate any negative feelings toward the Catholic church or its tenets. I did want him to ease his mind, which he did as we found that his anxieties had very little to do with masturbation. Repressed rage against his parents and a frustrated desire to control his own life (as he saw fit and not according to dictates from his parents) were, in combination, producing anxiety. The anxiety triggered the masturbation, he thus felt guilty, guilt led to anxiety . . . and on it went. So in Frank's case, an understanding of the dynamics involved helped.

THE FEMALE REACTION

Women, biologically different from men and without the need to ejaculate, sometimes do not understand the necessity for masturbation. While there have been old wives' tales concerning masturbation and pressuring from society for men not to indulge in "self-abuse," there has been little attention paid to women's sexual needs. Women have not been as chastized concerning masturbation not because it is *more* acceptable for women to masturbate, but because it has often been assumed that women are "purer," less sexual, and less driven by bodily needs. The women's movement and more enlightened thinking have made more people aware that women do have desires, that they are sexual, and that they do masturbate. Some women do suffer guilt in this area, but it is not as common, nor usually as intense as in men.

The particular problem that many women have with masturbation is not when *they* themselves masturbate, but when they are involved in a relationship and discover that their *partner* does. This revelation is for many people not only disconcerting but also threatening. Is her partner rejecting her? Isn't she providing him with enough sex? Isn't she sexually appealing any more? Why is he suddenly doing this? How can she get him to stop? Should she get him to stop?

Masturbation is not evidence of rejection. It may be part of a rejecting pattern, but not by and of itself.

She may, indeed, not be satisfying her partner sexually, though he may be delighted by the frequency of intercourse and may only be using occasional masturbation as a practical, quick and easy outlet.

Whether or not she has lost her appeal is a question only the man can really answer. But she should not assume that this is so until she has talked over the problem with her partner.

As for the "sudden" onset of masturbation, it may not be sudden at all. Many men continue masturbating all of their lives, long after they have matured. Perhaps they have done it on an infrequent, fairly regular basis, or only during times when their partner was unavailable. If, however, either a man or a woman consistently and exclusively prefers masturbation to mutual lovemaking there is obviously a problem worthy of investigation.

Sometimes a man may attempt to cope with transient impotence by trying to get better in touch with his own sexual feelings. From a purely mechanical aspect, masturbation offers the possibility of considerable control of body sensations and responses. It's a selfish activity inasmuch as it involves one person, yet it sometimes serves a highly useful purpose.

It is invalid, however, to assume that masturbation can easily become so gratifying that it can eliminate desire for a man-woman sexual relationship. This transformation rarely occurs, and affects only the most alienated and detached men. These are men who fear closeness, or men who are genuinely hostile toward their partners. Often by overindulging in masturbation a man is crying for help. "There is something wrong with me (or you, or us) and our relationship," is what he may be saying.

NOCTURNAL EMISSIONS

Nocturnal emissions can do just as much as the discovery of masturbation to upset a couple's emotional balance, but it's a much less general problem. A large percentage of adolescent boys ejaculate during sleep because they have the sexual potency and tensions of youth, and because they don't always have the outlets available to adult men. If they masturbate often enough, they generally, but not *always,* can lessen the physical demand to ejaculate. The problem is much less common in adult men, since most pass their sexual peak during the teens, and because they can relieve their sexual tensions through intercourse.

Over the years I've known two patients above the age of forty who were troubled regularly by "wet dreams." The key word here is *regularly,* since it is not uncommon for men to have an occasional nocturnal emission at any age. Nor is it a matter for concern. Of my two patients, one was particularly potent, and it simply didn't matter how often he had intercourse. The other patient, however, had a very unsatisfactory sex life, and when his sex life improved, the nocturnal emissions diminished.

Chapter 16

Pornography

> Pornography: Obscene literature, art or
> photography, especially that having little
> or no artistic merit.
> Obscene: (1) Offensive to modesty or de-
> cency; indecent; lewd.
> (2) Causing or intended to cause sexual
> excitement or lust.
> —*Random House Dictionary of
> the English Language*

What is pornography?

Pornography is difficult to define because what society deems pornographic changes with time, as do
other cultural values, definitions and customs. What
might have seemed outrageous as recently as five or
six years ago may seem harmless and even laughable
today.

Elvis Presley was introduced to millions of viewers
across the nation when he made his debut on the "Ed
Sullivan Show" back in the late fifties. A furor erupted
over the supposedly *lewd* way he swiveled his hips as
he sang. In fact, it was considered so suggestive that
the camera operators were ordered to keep the picture
above his waist. This seems ludicrous now, and in his
audience today, enjoying every minute of his performance, *including* the hip swiveling, are many of the
same people who were mortified by him not so long
ago.

By the same token, paintings that once were considered pornography are later accepted as classic works
of art. In literature, the same controversy has often

made headlines. D. H. Lawrence's *Lady Chatterly's Lover* was judged obscene when first published and is a classic today. And how many men would have carried *Playboy* magazine on the subway or bus ten years ago? *The Moon is Blue,* a film most people would find tame, even boring, was all the rage in the 1950s because it contained references to *virginity* and *seduction.* The list could go on and on.

Men, and women, often make judgments on the basis of their *own, private* concepts involved in an issue. This may be related to what a person "can live with" or what makes him uncomfortable. Before we discuss men and their feelings about pornography (and its impact upon them), it's important to understand that the critics and defenders of questionable material seem to alter their stands constantly—often dramatically—as the debate continues and the social climate changes.

Speaking only for myself, I haven't had too much success in forming a definition I would be completely happy with. The best I've been able to say is that pornography consists of material that is titillating *and* is primarily *and* almost completely written or produced for the purpose of direct sexual stimulation (as opposed to material that provokes sexual excitation—either blatantly or subtly—as a side-effect).

PICTURE OR PORNOGRAPHY

Men have always been clever in their attempts to satisfy their basic desires for sex, money, power and love. To get what they wanted, they have used every method imaginable, and erotic "art" has certainly served as a very useful means of creating sexual stimulation. Anyone who has ever studied archeology or the history of art knows that the depiction of sexual organs and sex acts dates back *thousands,* even *tens of thousands* of years to cave-dwelling societies in various parts of the world.

Pornography couldn't help but thrive as long as

the market was there—and it *always* was. It flourished in societies that encouraged it, but more importantly, it outlived cultures that tried to suppress it. So it seems that, like crime, taxes, death and the common cold, pornography is bound to be with us for the foreseeable future, despite any laws or taboos to the contrary.

Almost all men are at least *somewhat* curious about pornography. Interest ranges from occasional glimpses at a girlie magazine to devoted fascination with peep shows, hard-core magazines and paperbacks, and all the other "delights" up for sale to the devotee.

I know three couples who have done extensive traveling together and who in the 1960s visited the ancient Roman city of Pompeii buried during the eruption of Mt. Vesuvius in 79 A.D. In addition to marveling at the beautiful homes, gardens, tombs, municipal buildings and works of art in the excavation, the three men all found memorable a "male only" visit to a small room decorated with frescoes depicting an array of sexual activities.

A few months ago I reminded them about the story, and it took each one a few moments before he could remember that he had been so fascinated by the sex-oriented artwork. "Hell, I've got sexier stuff lying around on my coffee table these days than they had on those walls," one of the men remarked with some bewilderment. "Could I *really* have wanted to see that stuff?"

Not surprisingly, all three men had gone through the same changes of attitude as our society. What was lewd and disgusting and potentially exciting a *decade* ago, *now* is accepted as erotic, mildly pornographic and even amusing. Erotic "art" might not be lying on most coffee tables, or to be found in most homes, but I've an idea that tourists these days are much less interested in getting a look inside that small Pompeiian room than they once were.

Pornography, of course, doesn't attract only *men,* but not even recent cultural changes have prompted women to flock to its enticements. If you go to any porno theater, you'll see practically no women, even if the film showing was made with a female audience in mind. The whole business of voyeurism, of wanting to "see," is much more common to men than to women.

Pornography can be ugly and traumatic in its assault on our sensibilities. It can also give misinformation and add to confused notions and feelings. What takes place in a blue film usually has *very little* to do with reality. Ordinary men simply don't have the good or bad fortune to run into a multitude of compliant women who are extraordinarily expert in sexual matters and who at the same time have insatiable sexual appetites. These movies are not intended as true-life recreations, much less as documentaries, although many men seem to approach them that way. Some men make unfortunate comparisons to the sexual gymnastics on screen and to organ size, with consequent diminishment of self-esteem. But pornography can be useful too. In addition to its obviously stimulating effect it sometimes provides useful education. Indeed some medical schools use pornographic films to educate future physicians in the variety of sexual practices it is possible for people to engage in.

I must point out that to date I have yet to encounter any valid evidence that pornography results in perversion or sexual crimes. The latter are evidence of deep pathology and few if any people suffering from sexual perversion are interested in what we deem standard heterosexual pornography. Sexual criminals are invariably very sick people whose problems start in early life, and whose origins have nothing at all to do with pornography.

PORNOGRAPHY AS A HOBBY

Even in small communities where there is little public pornography (*i.e.*, theaters, book stores, massage parlors), men are just as avidly interested in erotic material. It doesn't require any more effort or special facilities to hide a sex magazine under a drawerful of socks in Manhattan, Kansas, than it does in Manhattan, New York. (We've already talked about *boys* who keep these magazines which, unless homosexually oriented or confined exclusively to distinctly perverted sexual behavior, reflect normal curiosity that will translate into normal channels in later years.)

Men who hide pornographic magazines or photographs at home and use them for masturbation frequently do so as an alternative to promiscuity with other women. Some want to sustain exclusivity with their partners, yet at the same time have an enormous urge to see what other women are like. Quite a few men, and some women, turn to pornography for added sexual stimulation. Many couples regularly read pornographic books aloud to each other as a part of precoital foreplay.

A man who carefully keeps the materials secret and hidden is sometimes fighting his *own sense of shame and guilt* as well as the criticism he is certain he will face if discovered. Any woman who doesn't generally project an air of understanding and compassion certainly isn't encouraging her partner to reveal his innermost ideas and desires in this area.

Conversely, a woman has to take into account a man's sense of values and understanding if *she* wants to share some pornography with him. If her partner is *genuinely* emancipated, she can tell him directly or in so many words, and he is bound to appreciate her candor. If, on the other hand, he believes in sanctifying and categorizing women, nothing she tries— no approach at all—will work. Any attempt that doesn't involve a long-range effort to change his *entire* sexual outlook is doomed to be met with shock and total disapproval.

CONCLUSION

There are some general conclusions we can draw about pornography, but not inflexible guidelines. Pornography *does* pose *some* dangers, particularly if misinformation substitutes for fact. The danger of misinformation threatens most viewers, but it is especially detrimental to those men who already are suffering from some feelings of sexual inadequacy. Although pornography features men with huge penises, most men *don't,* and *shouldn't expect to,* match up. Nor should they expect to be immediately and repeatedly potent, or surprised if women they meet aren't always ready and willing or in constant, desperate sexual need.

Other than that, pornography is not addictive and it does *not* create sex perverts or criminals. Sex crimes are committed by men whose deep-rooted problems stem from early-life, parent-child relationships, and not by men who read pornographic magazines or see "dirty" movies. Even though they may be embarrassed by their interest, the vast majority of men, to put it mildly, who look at pornographic materials are perfectly normal.

The real issue that should concern a couple is not *whether* a man likes it, but how *both partners* react to that interest. For better or for worse, they both have to share a man's image of himself.

Chapter 17

Compatibility

Thou, my companion, my guide and mine
own familiar friend,
—*Book of Common Prayer,* Psalm 55:5

Human beings are social creatures and need others,
not only for nourishment and growth, but for actual
survival. Our way of life is complex, and man is no
longer capable of providing himself with all the para-
phernalia for living. However, the farmer, the doctor
and the mechanic aren't the only people necessary for
life; a network of interpersonal relationships—particularly companionship of some sort, regardless of the
partner's sex or the intensity and duration of the relationship—is also needed. Some people search for a
lifelong mate, some for a traveler to share only a portion of the journey. Some men are lucky enough to
find what they want; some search forever.

It happens that over the years, one of the more
frequent questions I've been asked comes from single
women who are looking for a male companion (in
most cases a potential husband): "Can you tell what a
man is like *immediately?*"

No, I have to reply, unless he provides a blatant
indication, there *isn't* any way to tell at first glance
what a man is like. Not even psychiatrists, who train
for years to interpret and analyze personalities, can
draw any conclusions *that* quickly. The *only* way for
a woman to tell what a man is like is to have a relationship with him that lasts long enough to let her
learn what's beyond her initial impression. In short,
two people can't know each other until they know each

other, and a relationship can't be a relationship until some genuine relating has taken place. With time, a mutual emotional investment helps the partnership grow and develop.

Let's assume contact has been made and the basic relationship has gotten a bit *beyond* the self-conscious bravado and restraint of the first few dates. Perhaps it's gone further, even up to and into marriage. What I'll be discussing in the pages to follow may be as relevant to some women who have been *married for years* as it is to some who only have known a man for a short period of time.

It is not, as some men and women would like to believe, a general rule that sexual response and satisfactory adjustment occur instantly. Foreplay and intercourse *don't* necessarily lead to mutual sexual satisfaction. Patience and compassion have a great deal to do with the evolution of a relationship, and nothing is more important than *communication*. Great lovers aren't mind readers; they can do what they think is best, but they can't *know* if it really is good unless they are told. Moreover, human beings tend to be arhythmic, so that like two soldiers marching out of step, they must work to be attuned to each other's sexual schedule and intensities of desire.

Incompatibility is seldom due exclusively to physical differences in response or desire, and just about never to disparity in organ size. Remember that sex between people is an extension and reflection of how people relate to each other generally. Much "sexual incompatibility" will of necessity, therefore, only find a solution in a better relationship generally. Sometimes, for example, it is more valuable for a couple to find more areas of common interest (music, art, sports) than it is to tackle the sexual area directly. But there are particular areas directly connected to sexual disharmony which are worthy of attention.

Couples who find that they're "incompatible" are often suffering from one or the other's unconscious hostility. The sexual area too often becomes a perfect target for revenge.

Since the passage of time and repetition constantly threaten to chip away at spontaneity and excitement, all relationships, including sexual ones, need to grow in order to survive. In the course of coexistence, people will find imperfections, highlights and doldrums. Many men, however, expect *more* and actually become convinced that they've fallen out of love or have lost physical interest for a particular woman when their sexual experiences don't continue to reach the peak of intensity of earlier days.

Compatibility is, of course, the responsibility of *both* partners, though I've seen many examples where both members were trying their very best to get along and failed in any case. Why? Because they were unable to express their inner feelings. Many men and women consider discussion of physical likes and dislikes crass, mechanical and downright unromantic. For some men, it's not easy to be told that they aren't making love quite the way their partners would really like it. Obviously, since telepathy doesn't work for most of us, some sort of visual or verbal communication has got to serve the purpose. But, as if things weren't bad enough, some people try to discuss the issues *during* lovemaking, rather than before or after. I don't mean to suggest that the topic should be raised at the dinner table or while shopping in the supermarket; just not *during* lovemaking.

EXPERIENCE AND FREQUENCY

Men are always struggling to loosen that stranglehold of pride I talked about earlier. Henry, the rather shy manager of a Brooklyn dry-cleaning store, had a problem that troubles many men.

"I never was a stud type when I was a teenager, but I made out okay," he told me. "I wasn't different than all the other guys, so I did my share of bragging from time to time. Sometimes what I said was based on the truth and sometimes it was based on a good imagination. All of us acted like we knew *everything,* and no one had the guts to admit that there might be one or two things he *didn't* know. Meanwhile the girls we went out with seemed to think we really *did* know everything, which didn't make things any easier for us. I got serious with Suzanne a short time after graduation, and we started making it together. The thing is, she had slept with some guys before and she knew something about sex. Actually, I think she knew *at least as much as me and maybe more.* But that wasn't the point. Even if she didn't know *anything,* I still didn't know enough. I was plenty ready to be good for her and to teach her some things I had picked up along the way. There was no problem with that. Only I got pretty uptight when she started making some moves I had never seen before. And when she started suggesting that I wasn't perfect, I fell apart."

Henry was certain he should have been *born* knowing almost everything about sex and that some reading and a few actual experiences would complete his transformation from amateur to expert status. That baseless notion was confused with all the jumbled ideas about masculinity that he had absorbed from the day he was old enough to understand language. "So," Henry rationalized, "if I don't know everything about sex, I'm not going to be able to be a good performer in bed. If I'm not a good performer in bed, I'm not as much of a man as I figured I was or want to be." Obviously, anyone that entangled is going to find it *extremely* difficult to take even the slightest hint of advice, suggestion or guidance from a women. Men are complicated and have a need to be taught by women, but the masculine myth usually doesn't permit this to take place.

"I love Suzie," Henry said. "I love her. Isn't that the key?" Yes, it is *part* of the key and certainly a major component, but no matter how great the love, that ballyhooed extrasensory perception that love provides isn't sensitive enough to impart full knowledge of either technique or a partner's thoughts. Women

146

must contribute their sexual "education" to the relationship and must help guide their partners to greater mutual happiness, but most male pride requires the employment of *subtlety,* if not extreme delicacy. To put it simply, she must be the teacher, but she must somehow get across the point that her input in no way is meant to, or does, diminish his masculinity and sexuality. Even men who don't bathe adequately or who consistently fail to shave until a sandpaper stubble of a beard has covered their faces need to be told gently.

At the same time, many men have an impossible time conveying what *they* want. It may be embarrassment, it may be something else, but there are many husbands and boyfriends who lose the chance to enjoy the company of their partners in especially appealing clothing or perfume. Worse yet, many can't get themselves to express particular sexual desires (such as fellatio). There is simply no substitute for open, cooperative, compassionate conversation to convey mutual needs. Books cannot do this, and there are some which unfortunately serve more as manuals for *battle,* in effect instructing readers how to outwit a partner with assorted tactics of love, lust, foreplay, positions and postcoital techniques. Like pornography, many so-called instructional publications challenge and tease men with impossible, foolish and self-demeaning goals.

Of course as soon as warmth and fun are replaced by a score sheet and stopwatch, anxieties and phobias are certain to follow. Physical performance can't help but suffer. Again, the more a man *tries* to be "good" (whether motivated by inner pressures or the demands of his partner), the more likely he is to produce precisely the opposite effect. People shouldn't be made to strive for superlative achievements or even, for that matter, for the "average." *There simply is no norm for frequency and style!* What might be perfectly "normal" for one man—or one couple—is abnormal for another.

147

We've seen how *men* can expect too much, but there are women who do too! I've received a number of letters from women who expected to make love at least every day or more and interpreted less sexual activity on the parts of their husbands as loss of interest and waning love. I've also received letters from women who felt that their husbands were too demanding and therefore more interested in sex than in love or in them as whole human beings. One of the latter women defined "too demanding" as more than once every two weeks. Unfortunately, many of these interpretations cause considerable misery and promote further corrosion of relationships. Many of these rigid, false and mechanical standards have replaced spontaneity based on individual needs, feelings and changing moods. People who lack self-confidence are always frightened of tapping their feelings and trusting themselves and their individual needs. Instead, they come to rely on inhuman, inflexible, rigid standards and expectations fed largely by gossip and pseudoexpertise promoted in songs, films and books.

LOVE—HATE

Does there have to be an eternal battle between the sexes? I don't think so, though I feel that this "battle" invariably finds its way into many marriages where it continues to be damaging. But it must be remembered that mutual contempt on a sexual basis starts early. If we insist on categorizing and separating feelings, interests and activities as well as individuals themselves into male or female compartments and camps, we cannot expect obliteration of the battle between the sexes, however much each sex educates itself about the other in later life. As long as fear or contempt (and the latter invariably follows the former) exists for the other sex, there are bound to be ambivalent feelings of love and hate in marriage. While some ambivalent

148

feelings are characteristic of being human, they can be powerful enough to create sufficient confusion and conflict to undermine a relationship. The battle of the sexes and the social structure that separates boys from girls and men from women does not help in this regard.

MEN ARE ROMANTICS

In the process of differentiating themselves, as we know, some men avoid anything "feminine," such as love stories. The macho image *demands* fiction (and nonfiction) dealing with war, sports, action and masculinity from start to finish. Let the hero be a wonderful lover and wooer of women, but keep the love aspect tucked safely in the background. The main theme should not—cannot—be love.

I find this outlook sad particularly because it clashes with reality. This may come as a surprise, but *men suffer just as much as women* from the illusion that love is the be-all and end-all. Unable to face the fact that they think this way, they frequently ridicule women for believing that love will solve everything. Ironically, even the most realistic of *men* are generally incurable romantics who feel that love is the universal antidote. After developing a good love and sex partnership, they often are unnerved by the realization that all their problems haven't disappeared. And the blame, unhappily, comes crashing down on the particular woman they're involved with.

In keeping with this dynamic, men also respond *very poorly* to rejection after marriage. Sexual blackmail by women triggers resentment and sometimes enormous rage, if not infidelity, because it serves to cancel the myth of "perfect love." The low rejection tolerance of men *occasionally* leads a wife or girlfriend to fake orgasm when he is aroused and she is totally disinclined. But this can be a "remedy" more harmful than helpful.

THE FAKED ORGASM

To pretend or not to pretend is a crucial question faced by many women at one time or another. No one is *always* in the mood for sex or able to enjoy it on every occasion. Fatigue, a cold or preoccupation with a totally unrelated household or business problem can numb desire. A woman whose partner is obviously very much aroused and looking forward to sex will probably satisfy his needs, even if her participation is little more than basically mechanical. But should she go through all the *emotions* as well as the *motions?* There are arguments on both sides.

For some men, especially those whose vanity is easily wounded, faking orgasms is almost a kindness. Remember, however, that we are talking about a woman's *complete* participation (including feigned orgasm) and not just her life-sized imitation of a stuffed doll. I had one man tell me his wife "just lays there with her legs spread apart. I might have done better finding myself a prostitute. They don't show any real feeling, but at least you know that from the beginning. You'd think my wife was paralyzed or dead—and I mean *dead*—each time we go to bed together." Would he have rather she'd fake it? He paused, thought about his answer for several moments and then answered that he wasn't sure there was anything she could do to satisfy him other than to truly enjoy sex with him.

Obviously, this couple had a more deep-seated problem. If the woman was inanimate during love-making because she felt *no attraction* to her husband, there wasn't very much that could be done other than to see if they could try for a rebirth of affection. In this particular case the woman's problem dated back to sexual guilt feelings acquired in childhood. That discovery helped relieve her husband's anxiety about their relationship, even though it was only the first step in a long road to the sexual self-acceptance she had felt at the start of their marriage and then lost when girlhood memories took hold.

All in all, sexual lying is fraught with so many perils that I think the only types of relationship that may be able to withstand occasional dramatics are those that otherwise are very stable. A relationship that has more than the usual share of mundane problems will probably deteriorate even further if the woman begins to fake. Ideal or "flawless" relationships don't merit our consideration for two very solid reasons: (1) they *don't exist* and (2) if they did, there would be no need for any faking since everything from breakfast to bed would be "perfect."

Not surprisingly, the majority of people I've known who admitted faking sexual response said they did it in order to satisfy their partner's physical and physiological needs. Some even conceded that they faked because they never could achieve orgasm, regardless of with whom they made love. Of the total, however, only a minority felt that there was any danger in faking. I believe that sexual lies almost invariably lead to difficulties. Even for those women who make the effort in an attempt to foster greater intimacy with their partners, the threat to precisely that intimacy they seek far outweighs the possible—and probably temporary —gains to be achieved. Of course if a man has simply not mastered sexual techniques, some restrained education is in order.

I must repeat that in order to be intimate, you've got to be intimate. Real intimacy is based on closeness on all levels of a relationship, and there's precious little room left over for dishonesty of any kind. I once offered this opinion to a woman who was deeply troubled by both her inability to reach orgasm and what she considered her "duty" to make her husband believe he was satisfying her in every way.

"I was a virgin when we married, so I don't have any basis of comparison," she said very unhappily. "I just don't think I've ever reached an orgasm in all the three years we've been married. What am I supposed to do; tell him he isn't a good enough lover? I don't even know if that's true or not (on a practical basis, sexual difficulties of this kind must be viewed as a

151

team or couple problem). Look, we have a good life together and I don't want to mess it up. I am not going to kid you by saying I don't wish that I felt something better when we have sex. I *do,* only we get along well and I don't think the risk is worth it."

It was her choice to decide whether the risk was "worth it," but once she did, it was my obligation to tell her that their relationship would be even closer if they were more open with one another. That didn't mean she had to stare her husband in the face, smirk and blurt out, "You're a loser in bed," or "Didn't you ever learn anything about satisfying a woman?" It did mean that she would be doing a service to their partnership if she *carefully and thoughtfully* broached the issue of mutual help with a qualified sex therapist with him.

Women sometimes enjoy intercourse without orgasm, but help is certainly indicated and available for women who never have orgasms.

I feel for the most part that faking is destructive to both man and woman. It puts pressure on a woman to be other than herself. This is demeaning and depleting. For her it may serve to complicate an already existing problem and may make it more difficult to get required help. For him it is dishonest and serves as a separating device. It is obviously also a potential source of mistrust, anger and disappointment. All relationships require accommodation. As I've said earlier, sexual harmony is never perfect. If, however, a woman is chronically deprived of orgasm, then I must again stress that open talk with an expert is absolutely indicated and vastly preferable to "faking."

OBSERVATIONS AND HINTS

Though it's certainly important to know about the pitfalls, it's more important to know about constructive possibilities. We've talked about most of the following thoughts before, so let's put them together with a few added ideas and see how they look as a whole. Don't make the mistake of confusing them with *rules*, however. They're only observations and suggestions. Here are twelve capsule hints:

1. Sex education is highly beneficial, but sexual *mechanics* are far easier to learn than compassion and sharing, which require considerable growth and development as adults.

2. Sex can sometimes be loving, lustful or mechanical, exciting and extremely satisfying or boring and mundane . . . or a combination of any and all of these experiences.

3. There is no "norm," either in frequency of contacts or in intensity of feelings or response.

4. Periods of desire fluctuate based on feelings and moods, the physical condition of lovers and how they feel about each other at a given time.

5. People are arhythmic, meaning that since they don't have the same desires at the same time, mutual adjustment is always necessary.

6. Both men and women do get tired, moody and depressed and may not want sexual contact for short periods of time.

7. Pleading fatigue all the time may be evidence of hostility, dissatisfaction, fear, anxiety, depression, sexual abhorrence or physical illness. This problem is inevitably highly destructive to a relationship and requires professional consultation as soon as its existence becomes evident.

8. The most serious problems people have relating to one another are not sexual in origin. If these relating problems are resolved, sexual difficulties either disappear by themselves or are easily remedied by competent therapeutic experts. Problems are best viewed as team problems and are most effectively treated on this (as a couple) basis.

9. Men and women can profit by discussing their sexual likes and dislikes with one another *but* at times other than when making love.

10. Few people are good liars, so the *truth* usu-

ally will come out and then, because of the lying, the consequences will be destructive.

11. Reward and punishment have no place in an adult sex life. Sex as a prize, or its denial as discipline or revenge can only *destroy* a relationship.

12. Most human endeavors are aided by creative enterprise. Sex is no exception.

Sexual incompatibility isn't something that can be cured overnight. It takes time, effort and possibly more than I've had space to offer here. But this isn't a marriage or courtship manual. It is, instead, intended as a guide to a better understanding of men. A woman who wants to know her partner better will read and consider. If some thoughts apply, she'll make necessary efforts and changes, where possible.

The real secret is to *stop, look, listen, talk* and *try!* This does not indicate that responsibility for mutual problems is in any way the sole responsibility of the woman. Unless the man, too, is adequately motivated and cooperative, mutual problems in sexual, as well as other areas, can not be resolved.

Chapter 18

Tradition, Marriage and Beyond

> Marriage resembles a pair of shears, so joined that they cannot be separated; often moving in opposite directions, yet always punishing anyone who comes between them.
> —Sydney Smith,
> Lady Holland's Memoir I, xi

This world isn't the Garden of Eden. If it were Paradise, men and women would spot their perfect mates the first time they saw them. Love would be of the first sight variety for both parties, and couples would walk off hand in hand to enjoy undisturbed bliss forever after. There'd be no coyness, no jealousy, no little black books or blind dates and no heartbreak.

Marriage isn't always heaven, of course, but most men and women still consider it the most appealing and rewarding route to happiness and satisfaction. As our society has gone through changes, so has the traditional process of courtship. More couples are choosing to live together openly rather than wed, a decision that couldn't have been made with quite the same ease and frankness a few years ago. They remain an *infinitesimally* small percentage of all male-female relationships, however, and most couples who hope to share an enduring partnership opt for a legalized union. Still, even for them, modernization has made inroads.

How many women in the past were forward enough to make a marriage proposal? They might have pushed, pulled, lured and seduced their boyfriends toward the altar, but with victory just a few words away, the privilege of popping the decision-making question was left to the *man*. Despite what most of us think, legends of captured brides, carried off by their brawny boyfriends as relatives screamed and sped to the rescue, tend to be more fictional than historic. There's no denying that such abductions did take place over the centuries, although more as an oddity than as a standard of behavior.

At the same time, enough evidence has been found to indicate that many tribal warriors, particularly in Africa and some of the mid-ocean island chains, literally *picked up* a bride or two from the village of a defeated foe at the end of a battle. When men talked about fighting to protect their families, they really meant it. Once captured and forcibly wed to their new "husbands" (whom they had never met before the kidnappings), the unwilling brides were left to pray for rescue or to make good an escape on their own.

Would-be husbands had a problem of their own if they were part of the Sakalava tribe on the island of Madagascar (now the Malagasy Republic). To convince his prospective bride—or at least her mother and father—that he was worthy, he was required to stand across from a friend who would throw spears at him. The suitor would have to catch each of the spears in between his side and his arm, remaining outwardly unperturbed throughout the ordeal.

In the Caroline Islands of the south Pacific, the young men of one particular community were required by tradition to let their *mothers* select their future wife, make the proposal, prepare the bride for the ceremony, and then pretty well dominate the couple for years to come.

Today's man interested in marriage doesn't face quite the same threat to life and limb, even though many societies still insist on ceremonies that retain the symbolism of the bygone tests of manhood and worth. Combat on the battlefield has been replaced by combat in the office and at the factory. Pressures that once impelled a husband to forage for food or fight for the lives of his wife and children, now compel him to cope with many of the old problems as well as new ones, such as independence, choice, variety and responsibility. Living together poses similar, though lesser, problems. Men who are particularly detached will still find such an arrangement a threat, but not *nearly* as threatening as any kind of legally binding union. Men who are *not* detached will usually take quite readily to living together *if* they find a woman with whom they feel they can enjoy and share life. For the time being, however, marriage still holds no great virtues or rewards for men, and remains substantially more inviting for women.

For those who do get married, the decision whether or not to wear a wedding ring sometimes, though not always, gives a hint of more repressed feelings. In one regard, it seems almost ironic that women insist on wearing rings. In addition to its role as a symbol of union and—to some—of victory, *some* anthropologists believe it may be a descendant of the rings and bracelets worn by *slave women* in civilizations past.

Many men wear wedding rings for much the same reasons as women, particularly because it seems to indicate a certain level of involvement, esteem and maturity (divorce records might lead some of us to another conclusion). Men who *refuse* to wear rings have other reasons, not all of which they admit too freely. Some men find wedding rings *degrading,* others a confirmation that they've not only passed from adolescence into the adult stage marriage is supposed to represent, but they're now well on the way to old age. I've been told by some patients and friends that they regard their rings as a uniform that mocks their sacred individuality. Some have said the circlets remind them of their marital responsibilities, a pressure that has little, if anything, to do with the degree of love they feel for their wives and children.

I've already delved into the varying negative effects of pressure and expectation on male sexual response

157

and potency, so there isn't much need to detail how a sense of imprisonment implied in marriage vows can affect a man's sexual activity. Consider the expectations placed on faithful observers by the Torah, the Jewish book of laws. As prescribed, a wife could expect a certain number of conjugal visits, depending on her husband's occupation. The wife of a sailor could only count on sex every *six months;* a camel driver's spouse had better luck—once every *thirty days;* assdrivers were expected to produce *once-a-week;* and laborers *twice-a-week.* Pity the poor fellow who was unemployed. According to the Torah, he had to make love *every* day!

IMPACT OF A CHILD

The addition of children to a family adds a little something extra, both literally and figuratively. An eager, expectant father has to make many major adjustments in dealing with his wife, including understanding the physical problems that occasionally prompt a mother-to-be to abstain from intercourse. There's also a unique feeling of special warmth and love that couples experience when they consciously attempt to conceive a child. I've known many wives who reported that their husbands demonstrated an increased—and frequently *brand new*—tenderness once pregnancy was confirmed.

But, as always, there are men who react poorly to the prospect of children. Sometimes their reasons are purely practical. Perhaps they don't have enough income or savings to support adequately a family of three. They may simply not want to divert the time and attention from their private and regular activities, including those shared with their wives, to the care of a growing infant. Other men, feeling like children themselves (mostly on an unconscious level), cannot tolerate either the added responsibilities of parenthood or the feeling of sibling rivalry engendered by the birth of children in the family. These men cannot share their wife-mothers with other children, even their own.

Children are felt by many people to be extensions of themselves, and as the greatest possible strengthening of the marriage bond. A man with healthy self-esteem welcomes an extension of himself with happiness and increased self-esteem. A man who suffers from much unconscious self-hate views his offspring as a further extension of himself to be loathed. The man who is essentially detached and fearful of close relationships may feel terribly threatened by this further evidence of emotional union with his wife. This is sometimes experienced as loss of sexual interest following the birth of children.

Despite changes in convention through the years and the increased ease and rate of divorce, the family remains the basic and most important unit of human development and relating. How can it be otherwise when we consider the extreme dependency of small children? The fact is, the human organism requires a great deal of time and sustenance, on both a physical and emotional basis, before development adequate for taking care of oneself takes place. Simply put, this means that we need mothers and fathers to take care of us until we become old enough and experienced enough to take care of ourselves.

I believe that human beings, unlike other creatures on this planet, are not governed by instincts. We are capable of choice, and we are capable of a vast range of adaptations. This means that we can and do choose to live in many different ways with variety evidenced by the many cultures that exist and their diverse value systems and life-styles. But it is no accident that existence of the family transcends cultural differences and survives the centuries. It is true that we tend to recapitulate our own experience, and having been brought up in families tend to develop families of our own as adults. It is also true that we recognize the need of children for both a mother and a father, and for siblings and extended families (aunts, uncles, cousins), too. It is also true that in a compassionate and humanistic society, we can look forward to being cared for with love by children, should we reach a state of infirmity and dependency. But it's more than that! Marriage and family represent mature commitment in terms of caring and giving to another human being and eventually to still others, as children are born. This commitment, caring and giving mobilize our most alive, sensitive and ultimately satisfying feelings. This "family feeling" has the potential to provide maximum sustained emotional satisfaction on all levels. That it often doesn't is the result of neurotic problems. But, to date, there is still no other institution or style of life that proves more satisfying in terms of human emotional need.

The family also continues to be the only reliable potential source (despite limitations imposed by neurosis) of emotional sustenance necessary for full human development. By full human development I mean human beings who are capable of having the full range of human feelings, yearnings, talents, desires and above all the ability to relate with satisfaction, on a sexual level, too, of course, with other human beings. Interestingly, children brought up in institutions without parent surrogates, however much is provided in terms of physical need, almost invariably suffer as adults from a kind of emotional stunting, including blunted feelings.

It sometimes takes many years to find out that giving of oneself provides the best kind of getting from others. I don't mean martyred, self-glorifying satisfaction. I mean the genuine pleasure felt in feeling our own selves come to full life and fruition as we care and feel for others. Family life provides the best matrix for both the development and exercise of caring, feeling and giving. So I have no doubt at all that family life will continue in all cultures and for many centuries, perhaps even for the duration of the existence of our species. I also believe that the convention we call *marriage* will continue too, even if its exact form (in terms of legal formality) changes from time to time, because it represents commitment to family life.

Chapter 19

Infidelity

> Where there's marriage without love,
> there will be love without marriage.
> —Benjamin Franklin,
> *Poor Richard's Almanac*

Nearly all normal men are lecherous, at least to some extent. Most people are not repulsed so much by lecherous feelings or even intent as by poor style and bad manners. But what about infidelity? Most men like to look, and some go beyond looking. Many don't!

With due respect to Ben Franklin, adultery and promiscuity also exist where there is love in marriage. While society imposes its rules and dictums, it cannot dictate away the fact that men are usually stimulated sexually with relative ease. This facile response to sexual stimulation coupled with even temporary boredom, a need for ego gratification, a fear of old age and/or sickness, doubts regarding masculinity, outright, albeit unconscious, fear of homosexuality and readily available and attractive women, makes promiscuity and adultery rampant. Of course the double standard, which makes it more acceptable for men to have an occasional fling than women, has helped, too. Much, of course, depends on a man's level of maturity, the degree of his emotional investment in his longstanding relationship and his own early family history. Men who have had a strong and fairly constructive relationship with their mothers tend to greater fidelity with wives. The same is true of men who come from relatively stable homes and have good self-esteem. Mature men usually realize that women are not the means to enter a Shangri-la and indeed do not believe in mythical paradises at all. Men who generally have a greater degree of genuine self-realization and self-fulfillment tend to be content with the home life they themselves helped construct.

Men who do wander often do not do so for lack of love at home, though this may be used as a rationalization. Quite often the home scene has less to do with it than internal restlessness, as well as an inability to say no to goodies that present themselves. Some men are addicted to sexual stimulation, and however much they love their wives, they need constant new contacts to provide the substance of their habit.

TEMPTATIONS

As we saw in chapter 14, fantasies are usually never anything more than fantasies—imagined wishes in picture form. Many men refuse to believe that their childhood daydreams of perfect satisfaction and a perfect world don't really exist. Once they're married, they begin to wonder if they didn't miss the one great woman "meant" for them. Reality has *definite borders;* fantasy is *unlimited* in scope. Women, sex, life, everything can be altogether as fabulous as a man's imagination will allow. The grass seems always greener, the perfume a bit more seductive, the nightgown sheerer and the sex more intense. The husband goes seeking, looking for the relationship that will be "It." And then the next one seems like *it* will be It. And on and on the search continues, with fantasy always *one step ahead* of reality.

Loneliness sometimes promotes adultery, too. Men who are forced to be away from their wives for extended periods of time—traveling salesmen, for example—must abstain, masturbate, or seek female companionship to relieve their emotional-sexual tension. Often they only crave conversation and social contact. Unfortunately it sometimes seems easier for a man on the road to convince a woman to *sleep* with him than simply to spend a pleasant evening with him *chatting* harmlessly over a quiet dinner. Some men just can't relate to strange women in any way other than sexually. Further, traveling businessmen happen to frequent hotel restaurants and bars, often the favorite hangouts for women inclined to sexual involvement.

The same need that motivates men to find company when they're lonely is instrumental in diverting others to search for alternate sources of emotional satisfaction when a wife fails to fill the void or a man believes that she does. So many men are so dependent and insecure that they must have a woman to lean on and to count on. They need someone to tell them that they're a good and successful businessman, husband and lover. Almost all men need an emotional pat on the back and a comforting shoulder to cry on from time to time. It doesn't really matter if a man's feeling of lack of emotional support is based on real withholding on the part of his wife or on his immature expectations. In either event, the man is dissatisfied, and it doesn't take much to make him notice *another* woman's smile or timely understanding comment.

A woman who fails to provide her partner with sufficient support (and that includes showing genuine interest in his job on bad days as well as good) may be jeopardizing her marriage. Many women whose partners have strayed look for the most logical reason and sometimes assume that sex is the *one and only* possible problem. Sex may be *part* of the answer, but it doesn't *have* to be. To men reaching for emotional feedback, sex is a symbolic conductor for the psychological charge of an adulterous relationship with the "right" woman. Occasionally-wandering husbands are looking desperately for the *mother image* who will tell them how wonderful they are and assure them that "Mama's little boy" can do no wrong. Thus these *obvious* sexual temptations may on a deeper level be mainly non-sexual from a psychodynamic point of view.

GROUP PRESSURE

Matthew and Howard had been close friends for almost fifteen years. They were both forty-two, married, and each had two children. Once a week (usually on Wednesday nights), their wives would go off together to play cards, leaving the two men to watch the kids, eat some snacks, and talk. This went on almost every week, interrupted only by vacations, bad weather, or illness. With the kids playing in their rooms or out with friends, Matthew and Howard were able to relax and vent their feelings on everything from last Sunday's professional football game to that morning's overcooked eggs. Bit by bit, they began to talk with increasing frequency and enthusiasm about other women. First the comments centered on movie stars or a shapely girl they had seen on the bus coming home from work. Then the discussions became more specific and it soon became evident that both men were desirous of an extramarital relationship.

In the long run, Howard only transgressed once, but Matthew let one affair lead to another. A man's conscience is unpredictable, however, and it was Howard who came for help a year after his one-shot adventure. "I did it because I was feeling tied down," he explained quietly. "Same home, same wife, same kids, same job, same this, same that. I wanted a change and I wanted to get away from all the waves of responsibility that greeted me the moment I opened my eyes every morning. I guess I thought that an affair with another woman—with no strings attached—would make me feel better. It didn't, but that's not why I'm here. I'm here because I feel guilty about what I did."

Many men do what Howard tried, but few, if any, ever really find the carefree existence they dreamed of with such hope and optimism. Compulsive adultery is a symptom of deep-seated problems and unresolved conflict and obviously not the cure for an inability to face realistic responsibilities. Howard worked out his guilt and went back to his home, family and job with renewed vigor and spirit. Eventually, he loosened the reins on his friendship with Matthew—in particular, he tactfully avoided those dangerous and depressing Wednesday night chats—and began widening his circle of friends.

I was surprised, then, when I got a call one day from Matthew, who said Howard had suggested I see him. I didn't think it was the best of all ideas, but he insisted, and we met.

He was, he told me, still "successfully" sneaking affairs without his wife finding out, but the pleasure had turned to a grind, and he found the deception growing ever more demanding and tiring. Unlike Howard, who wanted a brief change of pace and an escape from responsibility, Matthew was running scared. He was unhappy with his wife as a sex partner because "after all these years she won't try anything new with me." The only alternative, he decided, was to look elsewhere. But there was more to it than that. Matthew still pictured his wife as an "angel" and found it difficult to press her to be more sexually adventurous. By leaving his "good girl" at home and finding a "bad girl" to experiment with, he tried to satisfy his divergent needs.

Matthew not only wanted to experiment with new sex techniques, he was in the mood to try new women, too—for "diversity," he said. And although he *refused* to concede the possibility, he was glad to test his once above-average bachelor ability to attract and win the hearts and bodies of younger women.

MEN AS COLLECTORS

There are some men who have serious doubts about their own masculinity and feel the occasional or constant need to prove themselves again and again. And there are still others who hold women in tremendous contempt and regard them as objects to be used sexually and then discarded.

This contempt often translates into braggadocio, an outlet offering self-esteem while gaining the admiration of those friends who put great stock in such things. Don Juan, the legendary lover, claimed a total of 2,065 *conquests* during his rather busy lifetime, but I think we can safely disregard that figure as a good example of literary license. Men who try to emulate him in real life enjoy making "collections" and look upon each of their short-term partners as conversation pieces. Instead of collecting *antiques,* they collect sexual *experiences;* some boast of the total number of conquests, others of the variation. They brag, that it is a way to live "the full life." But for many people, it's highly *superficial* and unrewarding over the long run.

The late Alfred Kinsey reported that he could find extremely few men out of the thousands he had interviewed who had ever made love to more than one hundred different women. But, he said, approximately half the men (and a quarter of the women) he examined said they had experienced extramarital relations. While I've seen the recent surveys that indicate that only about one-fifth of all married men in the United States commit adultery, I don't think there's any real way to determine either the number or breakdown by ethnic and socioeconomic standards.

There clearly is a good reason why so many men who *do* turn to adultery choose that route rather than divorce: it's less complicated. Adultery involves adroit maneuvering, while the breakup of a marriage can entail emotional trauma for both partners (some men continue to be in love with their wives even while cheating), tremendous expense, separation from children, loss of the "mother" who will care for the husband, public embarrassment and, in general, a host of unpleasant problems. On the other hand, adultery can ultimately lead to all of the repercussions already mentioned, and most men also have to deal with their own consciences while having outside affairs.

In some rare instances, a man may be married to a partner who is ill either physically or mentally. In that type of situation, divorce may be unthinkable (just as it is to followers of certain religions), and adultery may serve as a "practical" outlet.

PROSTITUTES

Not all adultery is committed with "ordinary" women with families and jobs of their own, who enter an affair in search of many of the same emotional and sexual satisfactions pursued by men. Quite a few men confine their escapades to prostitutes, where the threat of involvement is virtually nonexistent. Prostitutes have to be paid, and they don't provide the *genuine,* lasting personal concern and involvement a wife or lover might offer. At the same time, they *do* eliminate the demand to be a good sex partner (the prostitutes don't care) and to supply all the complicated psychological underpinnings a woman may ordinarily need.

That sexual prostitution is called the "oldest profession" and continues to exist is no surprise. Our culture encourages prostitution in many areas of living; many people neglect their real feelings and yearnings and prostitute themselves. In a society where *everything* is sold for money, sexual services are bound to be marketed as well. It just so happens that we put a negative value on the selling of sex, though I often wonder if we wouldn't take another look at prostitution if the term was used, for instance, to describe a salesman who sold television sets but didn't really believe in the quality of his product. But prostitution is a degrading occupation which demeans the women who find themselves in it; no matter what analogies we might make, it is in reality the utilization of a human being as an object rather than as a person.

168

Adultery, of course, seldom offers any real security or deep and lasting satisfaction. Most women are bound to discover their husbands' infidelity. Some men *want* to be caught, hoping that the transgressions will be interpreted as cries for *help*. Many need to tell their wives for absolution. A wife is, after all, a mother-surrogate and is thus used as a man's extended conscience. Many women resent this kind of exploitation almost as much as the adulterous act itself.

Of course women can be unfaithful too. When faced with an adulterous wife, a husband will react in any number of ways. Some try to understand, and others become murderously vindictive in an effort to restore hurt male pride. In our culture nearly all men and women react with enormous jealousy (sometimes envy) and often rage. A man's self-confidence is usually shaken, and he will often become anxious and depressed.

Of course there are partners who become terribly jealous even though there have been no moves in an adulterous direction at all. Jealousy is not a function of love, and jealous men are *not* necessarily more in love with their partners than un-jealous men. Of course, the woman or man who is not adulterous, but merely hoping to engage a spouse's attention through promotion of jealousy, is running foolish risks.

Jealousy is powerful and irrational, an emotion frequently based on dependency and considerable lack of self-esteem, as well as self-hate. If chronic, professional help is absolutely indicated.

It may be that François de la Rochefoucauld described it best in 1565, when he wrote, "There is more self-love than love in jealousy." This is particularly pertinent to men and their tremendous pride and need for constant reaffirmation of their self-esteem. But as I've indicated, there is even more *self-hate* involved than self-love. In fact, it's not really self-love at all, but rather severe self-doubt.

Jealousy sometimes grows to alarming proportions in neurotic men as they get older. Since their physical abilities slow down to *some* degree, some husbands begin to worry that their wives will turn elsewhere for sexual satisfaction. Some people may find it humorous, but I don't think it's funny at all to see an eighty-year-old man complaining that his wife, who is eighty too, is chasing after other men *or* that other, younger men are making "a play" for her. Of course, such a man is talking about his own loss of sexual prowess. That loss has caused self-hate, which he in turn projects to his partner by tagging her with attempted or successful infidelity. I have also seen a number of very old men who in their eighties suddenly produce a list of their wives' supposed indiscretions dating back over fifty years. I've sometimes wondered if this wasn't also a kind of stimulating device, a peculiar attempt to identify with the excitement of youth.

SWAPPING PARTNERS

Men who look for an opportunity to commit "legal," sanctioned adultery occasionally turn to the fairly popular option of "swinging"—switching partners in any and all combinations with other couples. The man may initiate the encounters, but he's usually the first one to be emotionally stung by the effect. It's all right for *him* to enjoy having sex with a friend's wife, but some men can't help but feel jealous if their wives have *too good* a time. Still others feel they can't keep up with their wives.

Exchanging wives isn't a new practice, however modish its current practitioners believe it to be. According to Marco Polo, husbands in eastern Tibet considered it wonderfully good luck if a foreigner slept with their wives or daughters. Eskimos were known to offer their wives to a friend for a night. In several parts of the world (the Hawaiian Islands, for one), couples exchanged partners when they visited one another. In our society, "swinging" is a middle-class activity that justifies each participant's desire for promiscuity. Most men who do take part first seek the approval of their own wives; if they don't, then the "swinging" isn't anything more than just plain adultery.

Chapter 20

Male Climacteric

Every man desires to live long, but no
man would be old.
>—Jonathan Swift,
>>*Thoughts on Various Subjects*

To me, old age is always fifteen years
older than I am.
>—Bernard Baruch on his eighty-fifth
>birthday

Is there such a thing as male menopause?

No . . . and yes.

No because men don't menstruate, and yes because
a kind of menopause or climacteric equivalent does
exist.

Every one of us would agree 'that women experience
a definite set of physical changes (accompanied by
emotional pressures) sometime during the middle period of their lives. All sorts of physiological shifts take
place, most notably the loss of the ability to conceive
children. Other changes occur as well, including hor-
monal alterations. The psychological effect can be
burdensome indeed, but even severe depression, which
occurs in some women, is eventually overcome. The
important thing is that female menopause is understood
and accepted as a fact of life. As such, most people
do—or at least are expected to—take in stride the
painful moods of menopausal women. In any case,
it certainly isn't a taboo subject.

The male climacteric is not really taboo, either, but
it is not understood by most people. That makes it

far more trying for the man who has symptoms but is unaware that they are part of a generally normal period of transition. Depending on the individual, the reaction can be slight, even unnoticed, moderate, or overwhelmingly severe. In most men it occurs between the ages of thirty-five and fifty-five, but it can occur at sixty or later and sometimes as soon as the early thirties. A man *probably* will be in his late forties or early fifties if and when he has a reaction, but he can fall victim almost as easily twenty years before the "scheduled" time. Much depends on his outlook.

Among those people who are aware of its existence, most believe that the climacteric is emotionally, not physically, based. Any physical reactions, they argue, are merely offshoots of the overriding psychological problem.

The climacteric summons up fatigue, headaches, moodiness and, sometimes, most debilitating and annoying of all, hypochondria. There are also psychosomatic problems—physical changes caused by psychological concomittants—which include such diverse effects as indigestion, heart burn, rapid heartbeat, urinary and respiratory difficulties and insomnia. Even more troubling is a new-found inability to make decisions (psychological). Self-doubt grows, especially with regard to sex. Sexual drive can increase, but usually takes the opposite course and may even lead to transient impotence and premature ejaculation. And it probably results from the fear, in a way quite founded, that youth is fading, never to be recaptured.

Menopause may be comparatively easier on women than the climacteric is on men. Male pride being what it is, this kind of reaction can be very severe, especially since, unlike women, men cannot use physiological changes as a rationale for their symptoms because there is no overt evidence of changes taking place. Whether or not significant physiological changes do take place is debatable, but in women cessation of menses provides ample evidence.

Interestingly, many men can pinpoint the onset of symptoms, which are often directly linked to psychological trauma to self-esteem (business reversals, for example) much like depressive reactions all through life. In some men, reactions take place shortly after a *crucial* birthday, that day being the one which in that man's mind is symbolic of decline and the onset of old age.

The way in which a man accepts changes and pressures depends on the type of individual he has been all of his life. Of course his partner's concern and devotion can be very helpful. Some interesting questions of consequence are: How accepting is he of his shortcomings? How has he weathered other emotional storms in his life? What is the bottom line of his frustration tolerance? Most men will react with varying levels of unhappiness or depression, but eventually will feel better. Sometimes, a new humility and realistic outlook will make things better than ever. Sometimes more severe, lasting consequences occur.

It is particularly important during this time in a man's life for his partner to be understanding, to realize that though he may be vague in stating his problems, they are very real. Occasionally, professional help may be necessary. There are some medical people who believe hormones are helpful for those men who are severely stricken emotionally. I, however, am very wary of such treatments because they have potentially dangerous side-effects. A psychiatric consultation may be indicated.

It can be very difficult to keep men in this phase of their lives from upsetting the basic status quo. Too many take radical steps they hope will solve their problem. There are men who use good judgment; there are others who use little or none at all. I've known many men who quit their jobs, sold their home and left their wives—in short, completely reversed everything they believed in and adhered to up until that point. A large part of this upheaval is caused by anxiety and depression, which result from the realization that they are aging. Unquestionably, the toughest and most important role of a professional therapist right from the outset is to prevent a man from taking the radical steps that will cause him to destroy unwillingly some of the best aspects of his life.

THE ENVY OF YOUTH

Sex is often the adult proving ground where men think they must prove themselves. Older men may be envious of what they perceive to be greater sexual freedom these days (they happen to be perceiving quite correctly, of course), but older men have often been envious in bygone days too. They're envious of youth, of those who have a longer life ahead of them and of those who they feel have greater sexual vigor.

Naturally, there are men who simply give up and surrender to the years. Even if they think they would *like* to continue to be at least *reasonably* active in bed, they're certain that they shouldn't and can't. Physically healthy men may have sex well into their eighties and nineties provided they haven't resigned psychologically. The men who do surrender to time transform their false beliefs into self-fulfilling prophecies. Some are older men who feel guilty about any sexual desires simply because they think such thoughts are "inappropriate" for someone their age.

I'm not saying that response and endurance will be the same as they once were, but every man has to remember that he had his peak when he was in his late teens and early twenties. Still, Masters and Johnson have released statistics supporting the theory that loss of the ability to obtain an erection is *not* a natural part of the aging process.

There usually are changes. Most older men will not get an erection at the slightest stimulation. And many do need a longer period of time to elapse between orgasms. There are, however, the advantages of experience, and, hopefully, of increased understanding and compassion too.

The equivalent male menopause affects sexuality in another way as well. Because of the many possible physical problems attributed to emotional fears, what a man does with his body (and again, what he *believes* he can do with his body) depends on his susceptibility to suggestion and fear. The man who tends to be a hypochondriac will often be *certain* that sexual activity would further shorten his life.

Heart attacks are more difficult to brush aside. Countless men become extremely terrified at the possibility that they will suffer a coronary occlusion or—worse yet, if they've already had one—have another. That dread can affect everything they do, from the effort they expend at work to the energy they are willing to put out on the tennis court or golf course. Some men eliminate *all* physical activity, even if assured by their physicians that such activity would be more advantageous than harmful.

Rollo had that sort of problem, and for a reason quite familiar to specialists in the field of psychiatry. He had suffered a mild heart attack when he was forty-four years old, and it was more than enough to give him a paralyzing cardiac phobia. To try to insure that he would not suffer a repeat attack (an impossible task; you can lessen the risk but never assure such a thing), he cut back on all his activities, including sex. His career was unaffected because everyone he worked with assumed that his doctor had ordered the slow-down, but his marriage floundered badly. Disturbed by the cutback in sex, his wife spoke to the physician and was told rather conclusively that there was no need for any lasting slowdown. In fact, she was informed, some cardiologists feel sex is a wonderful exercise. When she confronted Rollo with that report, he became irrational. A few weeks later, he came to see me.

"I'm so scared that I'll have another attack," he

said, and he meant every word. "When you come that close to dying, you realize that life is a valuable commodity and shouldn't be toyed with. I've stopped toying."

In a few sessions, I found that, like many men, he had other motives in mind. Although he *was* cutting down on his vocational and sexual activities in order to avoid another coronary, he was also slowing down because he was certain that it was *too much enjoyment* that had led to his attack in the first place! Sex was too much fun, and he was being punished for enjoying it the way he did. To prevent a second attack —to appease the wrath of the gods, as it were—he would deprive himself of pleasure. While he didn't suffer a repeat attack, he did eventually grow very unhappy with the status of his marriage and career. We worked long and hard (he was aided tremendously by his wife), and eventually he returned to a more active business and sex life.

FEAR OF DEATH

Some sicknesses are avoidable. Death isn't. And though we all must die, we do not have to live our lives obsessed by the fear of death. Franklin D. Roosevelt said, "All we have to fear is fear itself," but centuries before, Publius Syrus wrote, "The fear of death is more to be dreaded than death." "Despise death," he also advised, "and you have conquered every fear."

The moment of death is *not* the worst time in a man's life. The point at which he realizes that it will, without any doubt, happen to *him* is much more distressing. Children know death as a word. As they grow, it becomes a concept and something that happens to *other* people and will "someday" happen to them, too. Some men go into their thirties and even forties with a childlike notion that somehow, through some incredible magic, they will escape death. When the full consciousness of inevitability does hit, it does so fast and hard. And then it sometimes lingers on destructively.

The only thing a man can do is to learn to cope with this most human of all realizations and to use the here and now to its fullest advantage—not an easy adjustment at all. To deal with the situation, some men withdraw into depression and resignation, choosing to "wait" for the inevitable, no matter how many years away it may be. They begin to feel dead before their time, and this can easily lead to impotence. If the issue isn't resolved before it worsens, temporary impotence can rapidly become chronic.

Again, a man who attempts to recapture his own youth by leaving his wife and starting a new family with another, much younger woman, is also in a battle against death. On an unconscious level, he is literally, as well as figuratively, trying to re-create himself by having another child. It is for him a kind of reincarnation *before* death.

Can a woman allay her partner's fears? Not all that much, really, except by being supportive and responsive to his sexual desires. The climacteric is a low point in a man's life, when he needs reassurance and as much ego gratification as his partner can possibly give him. Encourage him, because by doing so you may help him with his confidence. You may also help to watch that he doesn't go overboard in his pilgrimage to the Fountain of Youth.

Chapter 21

The New Woman

Equality is the chief groundwork of equity.
—Montaigne, *Essays* I, xix

The widespread women's movement is a relatively new phenomenon in the United States, even though the history books describe strong and occasionally successful efforts mounted as early as the mid-nineteenth century. The wearying campaign that finally won women the vote was certainly the highlight, but in the overall context of continuing reform attempts, it was a grain on a vast and sandy beach. Nowadays, changes occur more often *and* more rapidly.

New technological advancements are announced almost every week, and mass communication can sweep a new idea and concept across the nation and throughout the world in the same time it used to take to advance from one hamlet to the next. People move with enormous speed too—by jet planes, cars and all the other modern travel conveniences. Still, with an endless list of ingenious advancements to his credit, man has been unable to adjust one object to the superspeed tempo—himself. He wants changes, often for good reasons, sometimes merely for the sake of change. He wants change fast, faster, faster, and faster yet! But *some* things he is reluctant to change; *some* things he is afraid to change; *some* things he hopes will never change.

Of course women *do* deserve and need complete equality and opportunity. They *do* deserve to be viewed as human beings before they are viewed as women, and yet countless men have difficulty with both the idea that women are not simply their adjuncts but their partners, and with the realization that women have needs (and the *right* to fulfill those needs) that frequently run counter to masculine desires and expectations. Fear of change and fear of unfamiliarity continue to impede progress. I have no doubt at all, though, that we are moving in the direction of complete equality and that women's increasing influence and contribution will make a better life for all human beings.

THE MALE: ADDED EXPECTATIONS

Before Freud (followed by Dr. Kinsey and other knowledgeable sex researchers), no one really knew what constituted good, poor, excellent or average sexual behavior. Virtually all "grades" were subjective, since there really were no substantial scientific statistics and research to support one theory or another. As we saw in the chapter on impotence, absence of these criteria and the general belief that women are not supposed to enjoy sex but only participate in order to procreate and to please their partners meant there was little, if any, pressure on men to perform sexually. When they were ready for sex, they made their move. When they weren't ready, hardly a woman dared (or even thought of) questioning them.

Today, many women realize that they are not only entitled to sexual gratification, but have just as much right and justification as men for acting as the initiators. Too many men, however, find this frightening.

The new attitude does not just appear out of midair, of course. Birth control has freed women from the fear of unwanted pregnancy. This and liberalized abortion laws have provided an alternative to having an unwanted child. Relief from puritanical and Victorian attitudes about many things has gone a long way (but certainly not yet far enough) toward giving women equal access to the benefits—and responsibilities—enjoyed and endured by men for so many thousands of years.

The psychological pressures that the feminist movement has imposed affect women as well as men. Both sexes find it confusing and anxiety-provoking to ponder societal roles and to realize that they aren't what they *should* be (or *could* be). Depression is not an unusual side-effect when self-examination suggests that values and standards have to be altered, but there isn't any way to avoid such growing pains. Ultimately, the whole drawn-out evolution will lead to greater liberation for *both* sexes. Boys, after all, do learn from their mothers, their sisters and eventually, their wives. "Liberation" will free women of the tangled view of masculinity, and as a consequence, help relieve men of its burden. How much easier it will be for men to live without the myth of masculinity forcing them to alienate themselves from women, to repress feelings, and to live the glorified macho life.

For the moment, though, women's changing and evolving role causes chaos in many quarters. Men *are* dependent on women, as we've seen, and they are dependent on a kind of stability that has been there for as long as they can remember. Can anyone blame them for wanting things to remain the same? They are accustomed to certain feminine stereotypes, and are reluctant to give them up. When the scales that govern the balance of power in a household threaten to shift, most men panic emotionally.

TOWARD A GREATER UNDERSTANDING

Still and all, some women must come to the realization that they can't have the best of *both* worlds; if they want to achieve equality, they have to climb down from that lofty pedestal onto which their partners (and sometimes they themselves) have put them. The sooner a woman convinces her husband or boyfriend that she does not want to be idealized, the sooner he will see that she is as down-to-earth as he is and is neither a goddess nor a streetwalker. Ideally, perhaps, we would respond to the question "What are you?" not with "I am a *man*" or "I am a *woman*" but with "I am a *person!*" Maleness and femaleness then become of secondary importance, while being whole human beings retains primacy. Feelings of chauvinism or subservience about one's sex are equally sick attitudes and prove nothing (except lack of self-esteem). There is an increasing realization that there isn't all that much difference between men and women, and that those differences—physiological for the most part—are small indeed. As people we have infinitely more in common than we have in contrast.

Women are usually more attracted to men than men are. Men are usually more attracted to women than women are. But we both share the same sea of human feelings. When we don't, it's only because we have learned otherwise, and not because of inherent biological differences.

Matriarchal versus Patriarchal

History is full of examples of societies that at one time or another gave most privileges to the women instead of to the men. In a matriarchal culture, women made the decisions, owned the property and did much of the labor. Someone once observed that the difference between a matriarchal and patriarchal society is that the woman-based community emphasized labor by the landowners and ruling class, while the man-based community pushed the workload off on the "lower" classes and slaves.

Our society is still at least ostensibly a patriarchal one, and there are as many women as men who fear altering this structure. I say ostensibly because again we must remember that women exert the greatest influence on men through bringing up their own sons. For example, for a long time I have felt and continue to feel that if mothers brought their sons up differently, no man would ever go off to war. If women were not male chauvinists themselves, but saw themselves in an equal light, their sons would inevitably grow up enlightened in this regard too.

As women become more aware of their ability to express themselves on a sexual basis (and not be ashamed by that expression), they will, of course, risk missteps that can threaten their partners and their relationships as a whole. Many men are so frightened by new attitudes that they become sexually anesthetized. "She wants so much now and I can't give her all she expects!" they are saying. The danger is that some terrified men will flee anxiety, becoming impotent, celibate and in some cases even homosexual depending on background. But others will learn to live fuller lives with new outlooks they can *share* with their partners.

Epilogue

The mind is slow in unlearning
what it has been long in learning.
                    —Seneca, "Troades 633"

We've covered quite a lot in this close-up look at the psychology of men and sex. We've explored much and probably left much unexplored, but whether we've probed inquisitively into machismo, masturbation, fantasies or homosexuality, our journey led us to one inescapable conclusion: No matter how they deny it, no matter what they say or what they do, men are vulnerable, dependent, emotional human beings who need partners willing to provide love, understanding and gentle patience.

I won't pretend to believe that by reading this book *every* woman will be able to resolve problems that affect her partner and herself. For those who find that all efforts fail, I can't recommend too strongly that some type of professional assistance be sought. It may be a marriage counselor or sex therapist, or it may just be the family physician. But talk it out—communicate: I don't really suggest relying on friends or relatives; they're too close to the problem and may become upset about it themselves. Moreover, they aren't very likely to risk hurting your feelings by telling you what they actually think, if they feel you may not like the truth.

Before you turn elsewhere, however, turn to yourself and to your partner. Be kind, listen, exchange desires and dislikes, share, care and remember that men are not only struggling to overcome their own personal inhibitions, they're wrestling with the myth that has shackled the "stronger sex" since time began. Lord Chesterfield wrote in 1748:

Wear your learning, like your watch, in a private pocket; and do not pull it out and strike it, merely to show that you have one. If you are asked what o'clock it is, tell it; but do not proclaim it hourly and unasked, like the watchman.

Good luck.